At The Races

Photography by
LEO TOUCHET

Photographs at horse race tracks in Europe and North America

At The Races
Photography by Leo Touchet

Design: Leo Touchet

Type: Garamond

All content except back cover photo
Copyright © 2018 Leo Touchet
All Rights Reserved

ISBN-13: 978-1-7324433-1-0

First Edition
July 2018

Back Cover Photo
Copyright © 2018 Danley C. Romero
www.romeroandromerophotography.com

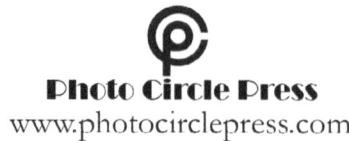

www.photocirclepress.com

The Horse Races

While in Paris in 1972, Alain Tartavel, a fellow photojournalist invited me to join him at the Paris Longchamp Racecourse, the birthplace of flat races. The big race that day was the Prix de l'Arc de Triomphe race which was then considered to be the greatest horse race in the world.

I had never photographed at a race track, nor had any prior knowledge of horse racing other than attending local race tracks and placing two dollar bets on unknown horses. Fortunately that day, I brought my camera bag along and attempted to photograph the horses in the earlier races. Not having the proper equipment to photograph the actual races, I took out my Leica M3 and began photographing the people in the grandstands and in the owner's circle.

When photographing people on the streets, I always had to avoid being noticed before taking a photograph. At the race tracks the fans were so involved with the races that they seldom realized they were being photographed. I could stand directly in front of them and photograph continuously during each race.

After returning to the U.S., I started photographing at race tracks in North America. The first U.S. race track was Saratoga Race Course in Saratoga Springs, New York for the running of the Travers Stakes race. That day in 1973, Secretariat was saddled and paraded for the fans to see the first Triple Crown winner in 25 years. Saratoga Race Course is the oldest horseracing venue in the United States.

The photographs in this book are from: Longchamps Racecourse (France: Hippodrome de Longchamp), Saratoga Race Course (New York), Evangeline Down Race Track and the New Orleans Fairgrounds (both in Louisiana), Exhibition Park/Hastings Race Track (Vancouver, B.C., Canada).

I'd like to acknowledge the from my wife, Elizabeth Burk and Lydia Smith, who accompanied me while I was photographing the races.

Leo Touchet

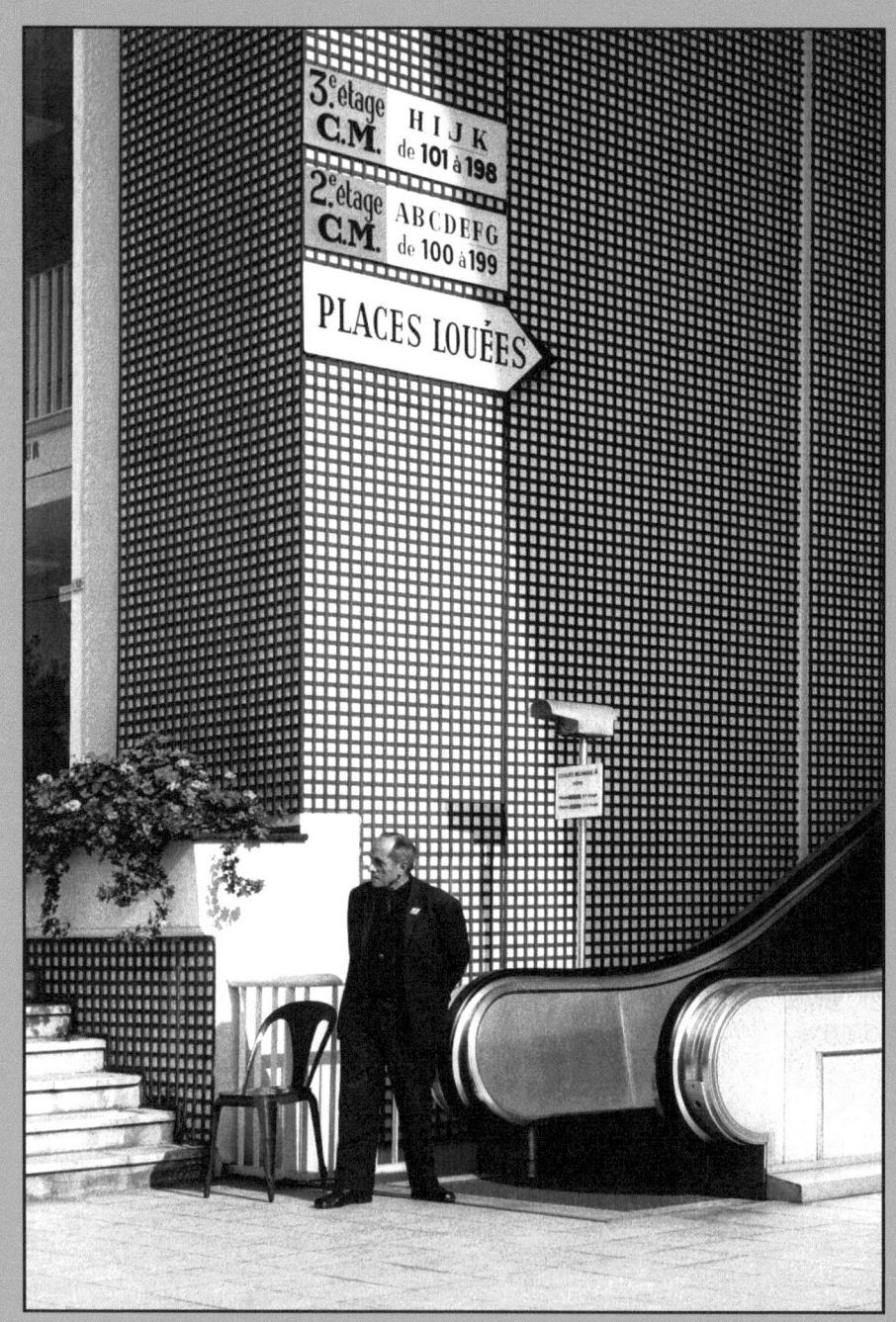

Paris, France - Longchamp Racecourse 1972

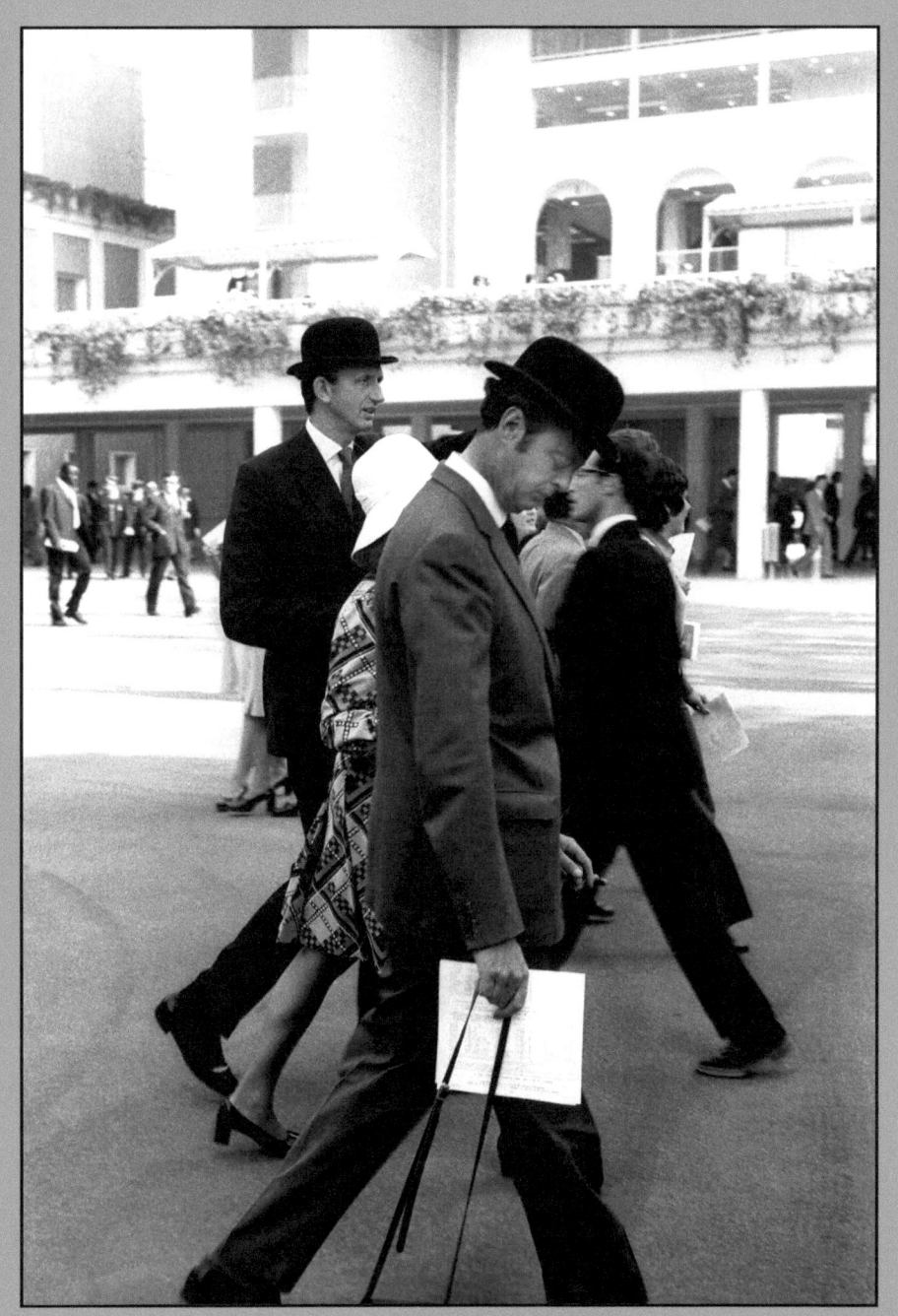

Paris, France - Longchamp Racecourse 1972

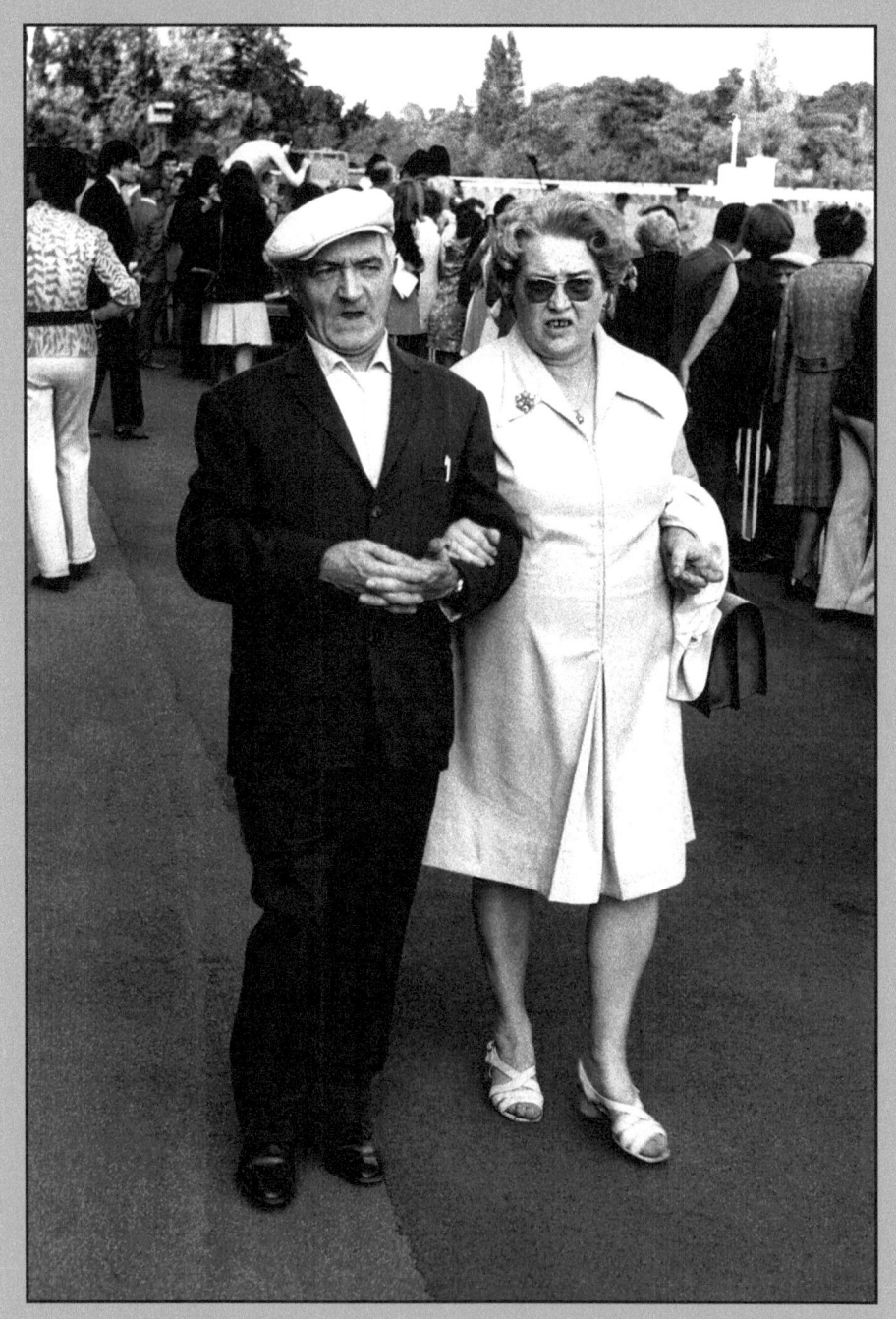

Paris, France - Longchamp Racecourse 1972

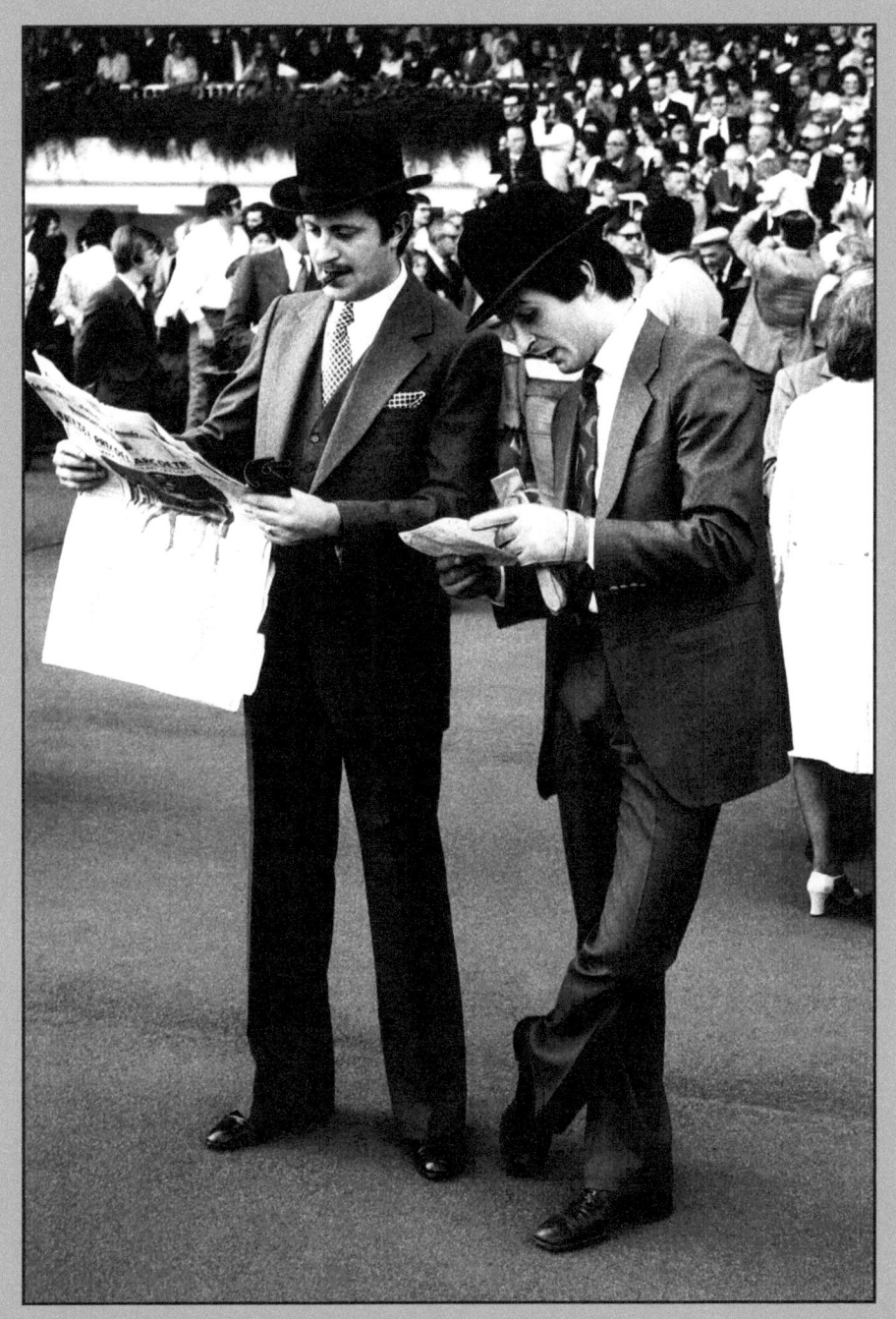

Paris, France - Longchamp Racecourse 1972

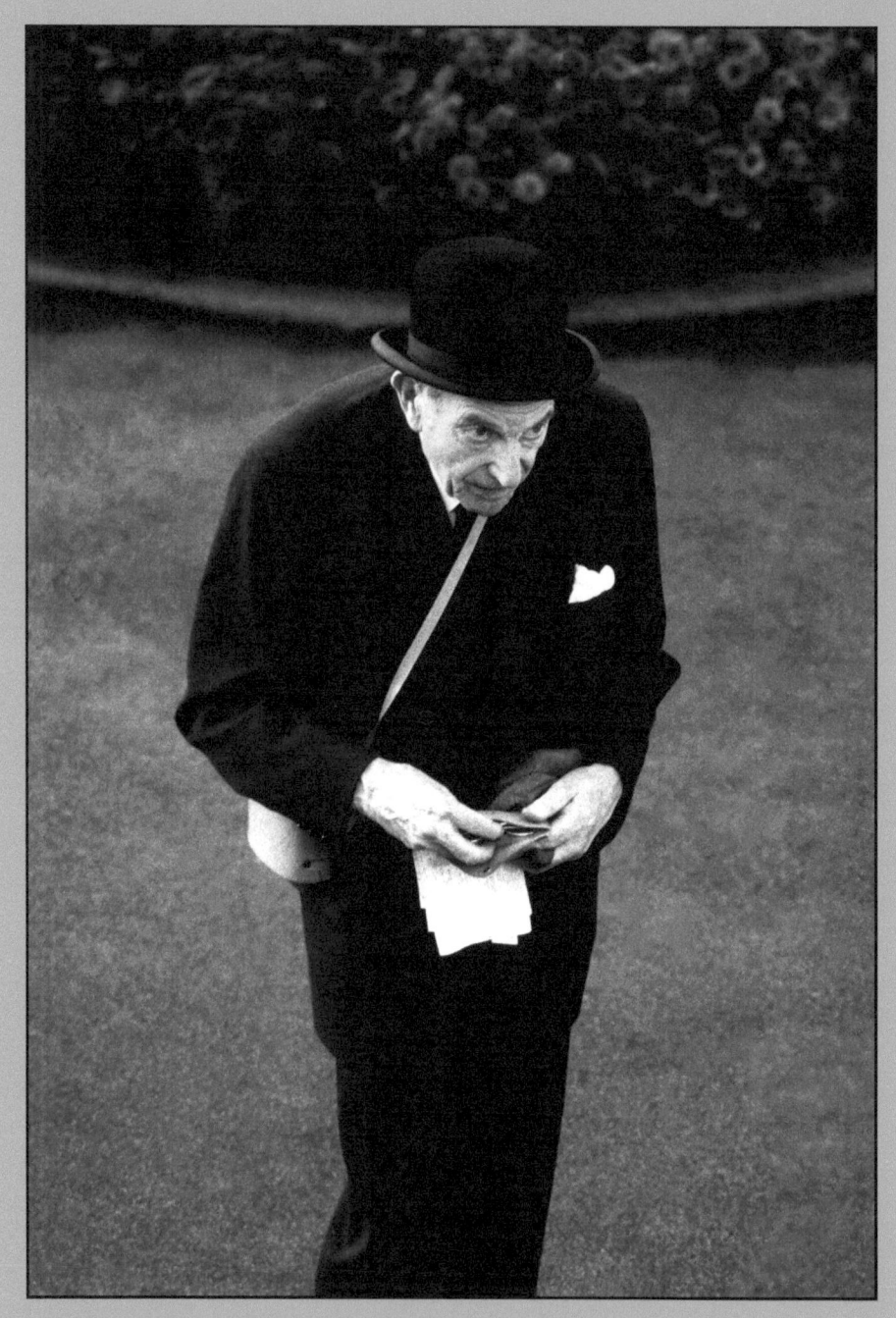

Paris, France - Longchamp Racecourse 1972

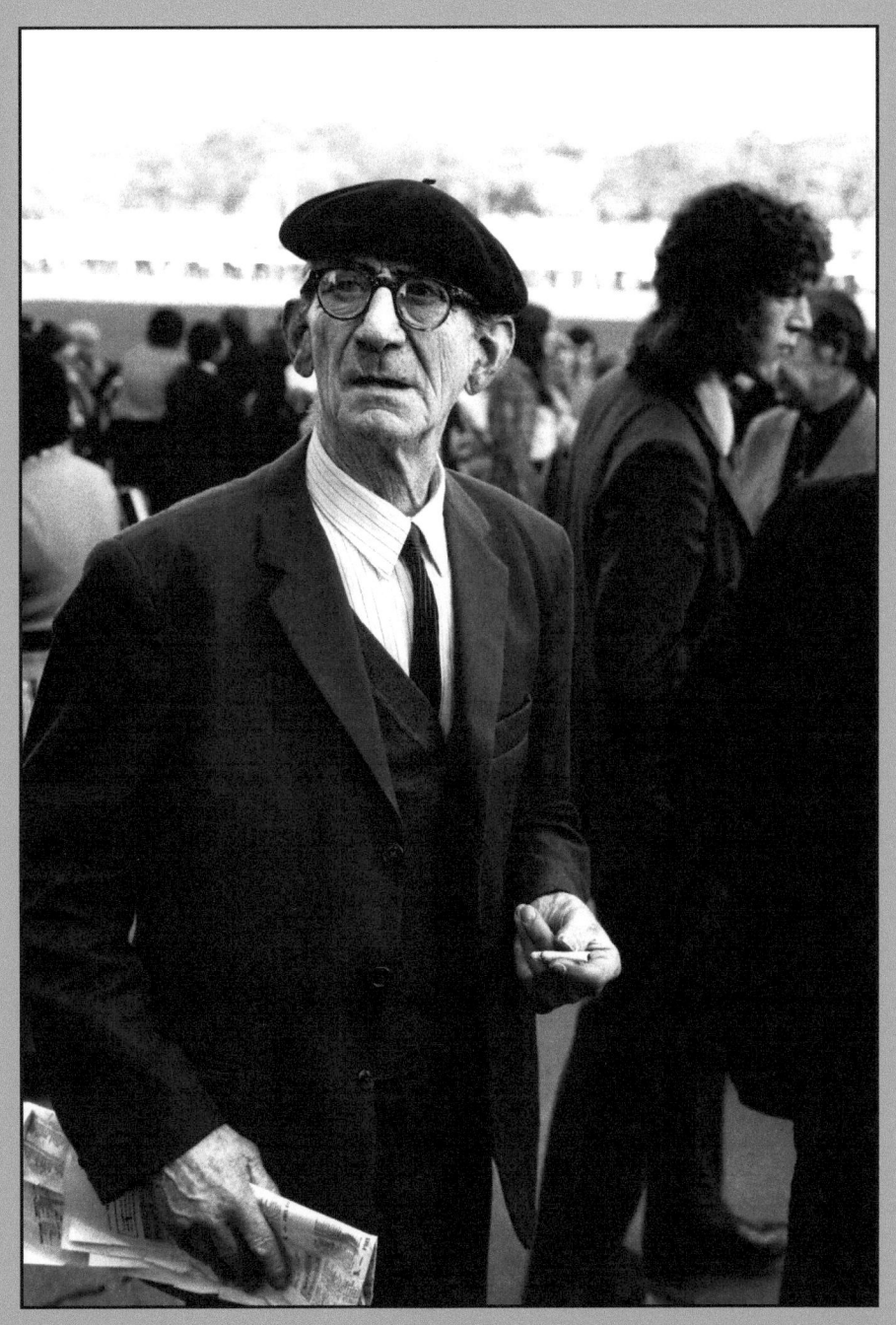

Paris, France - Longchamp Racecourse 1972

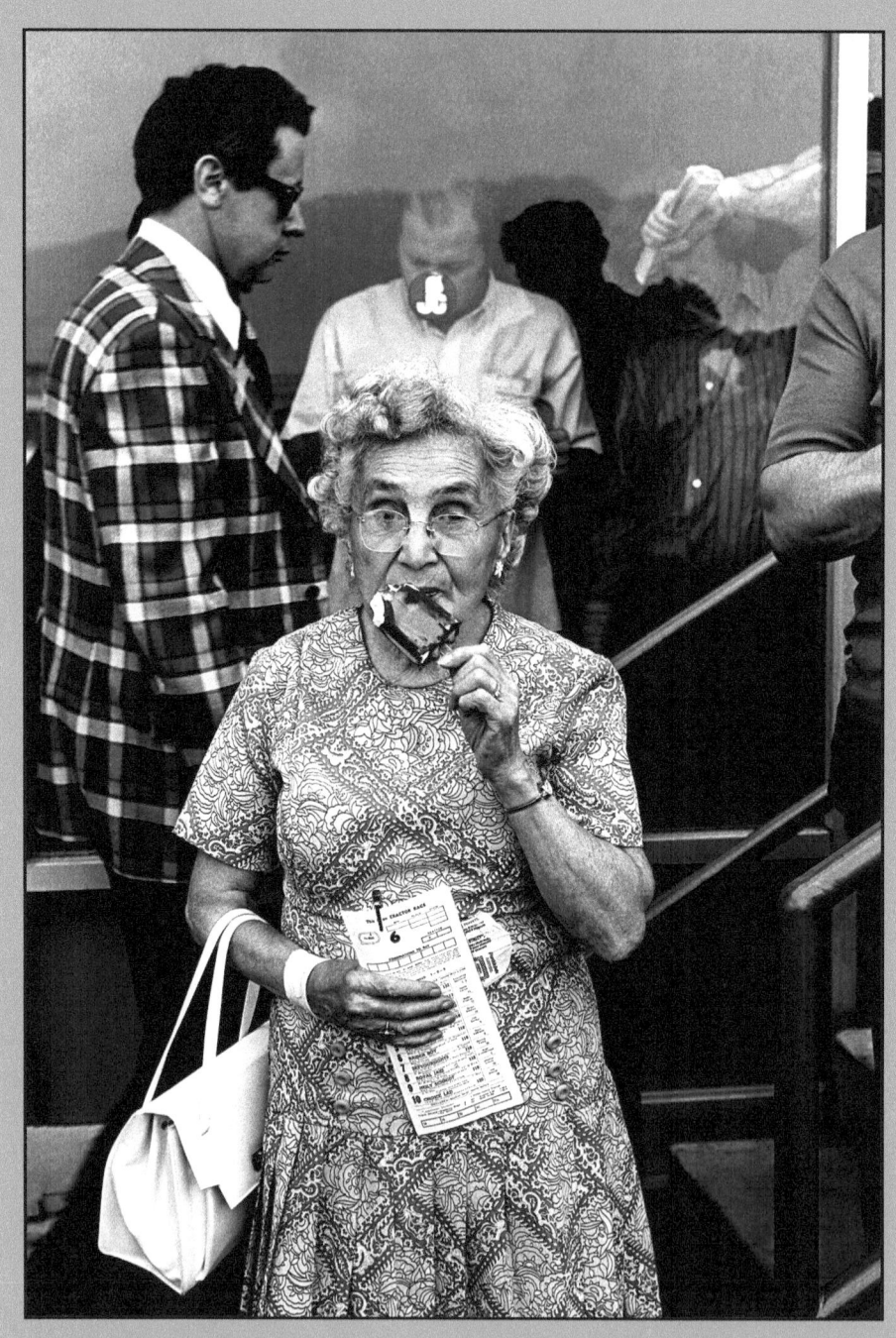

Vancouver, B.C., Canada - Exhibition Park/Hastings Racecourse 1973

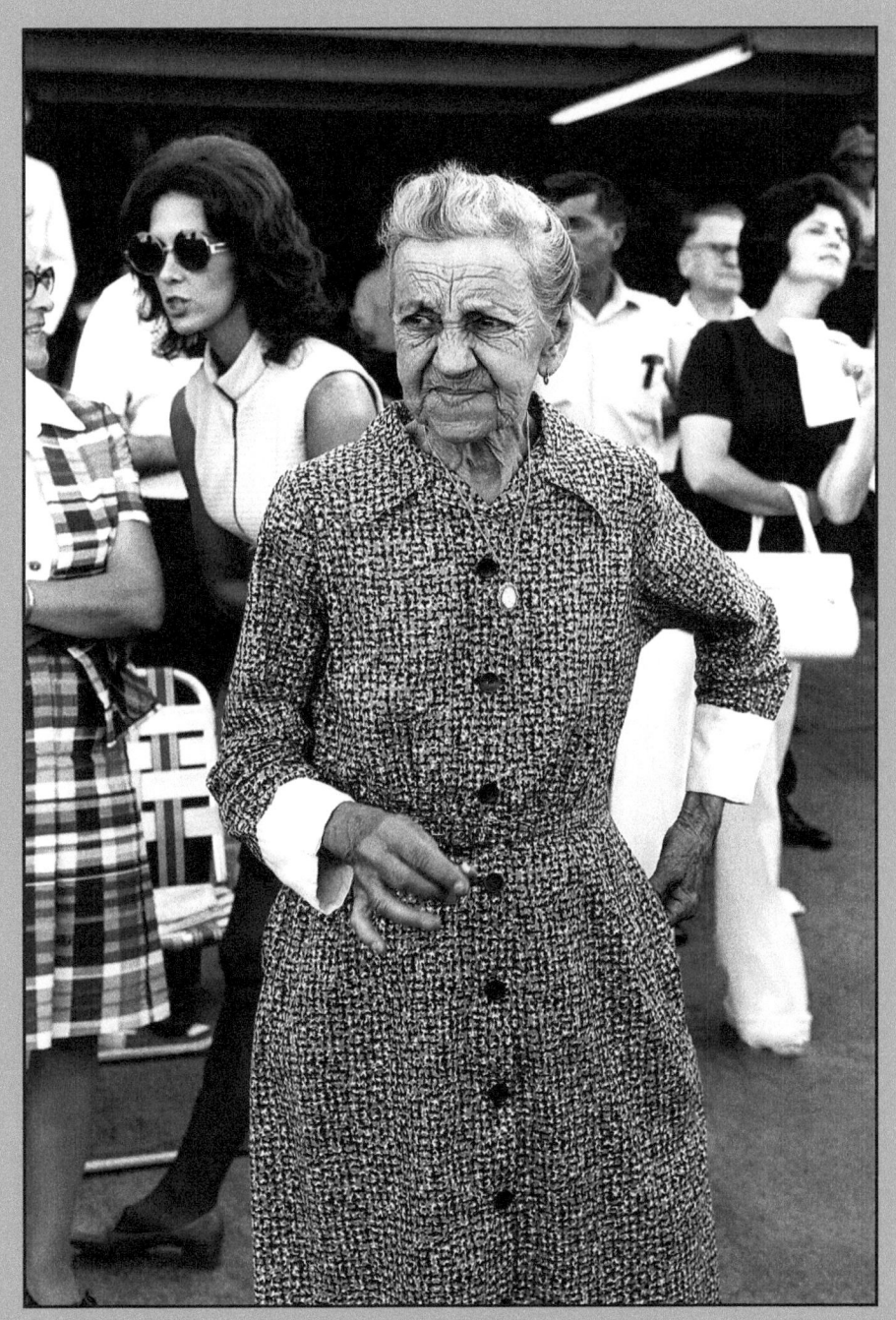

Lafayette, Louisiana - Evangeline Downs Race Track 1973

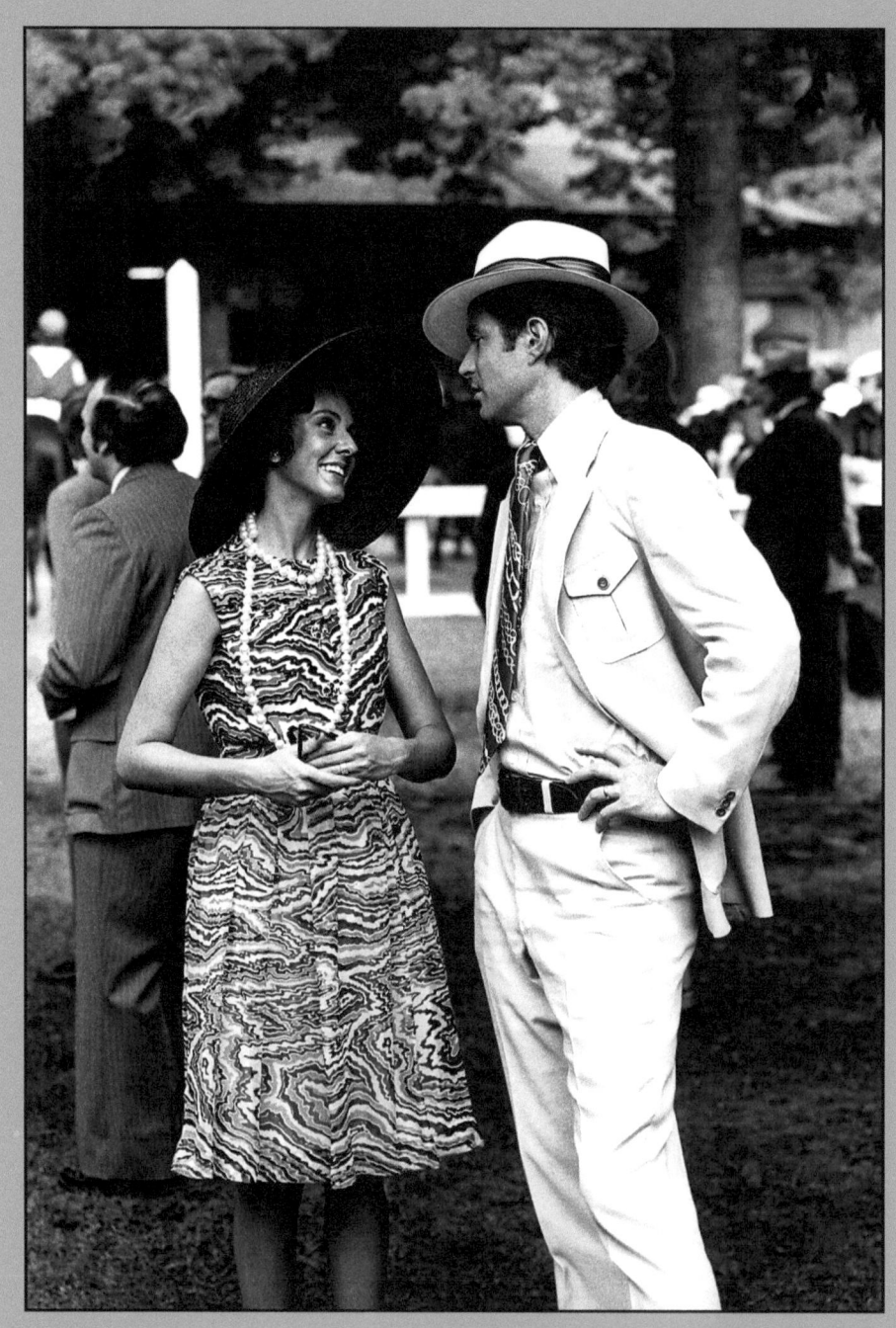
Saratoga Springs, New York - Saratoga Race Course 1973

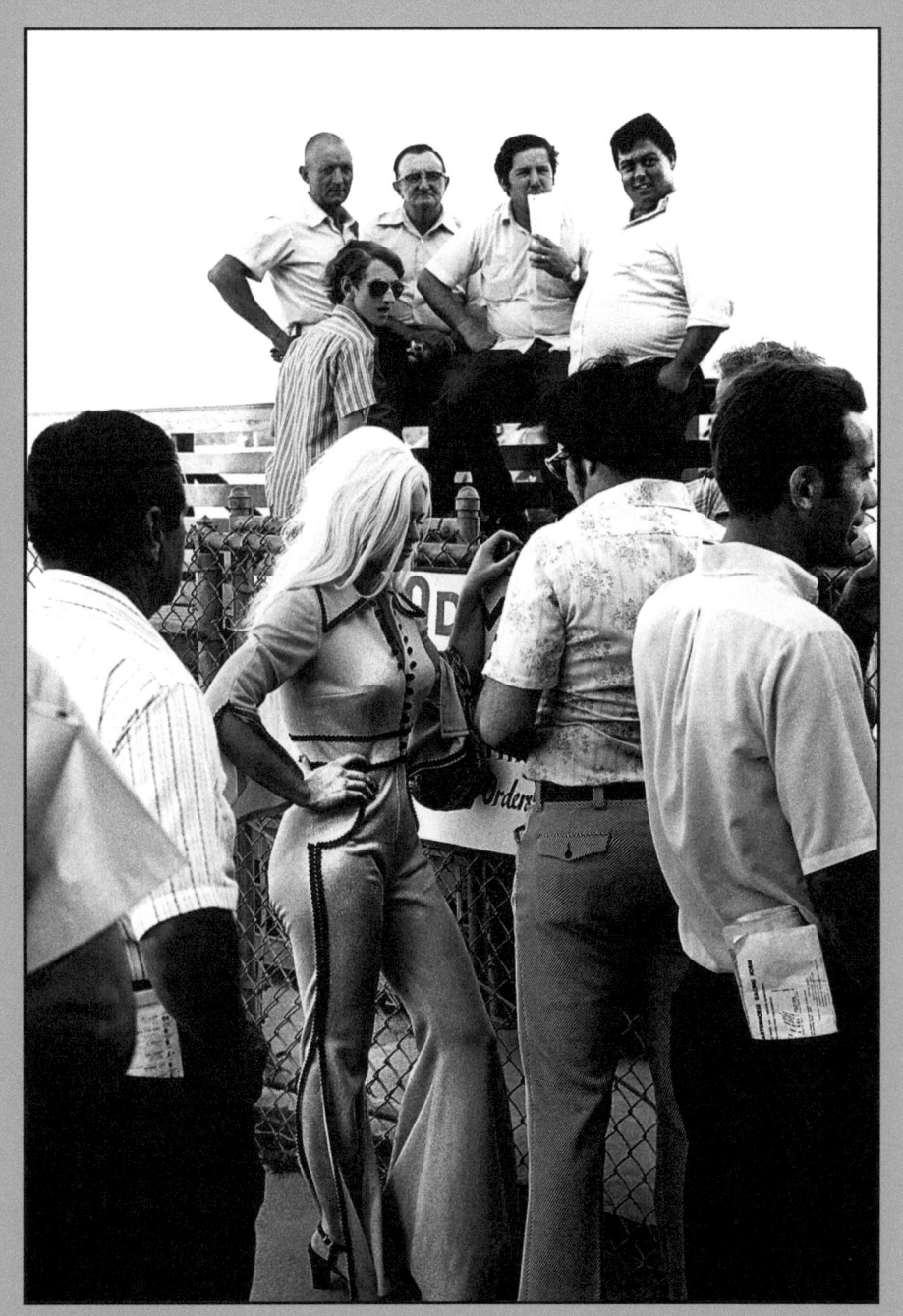

Lafayette, Louisiana - Evangeline Downs Race Track 1973

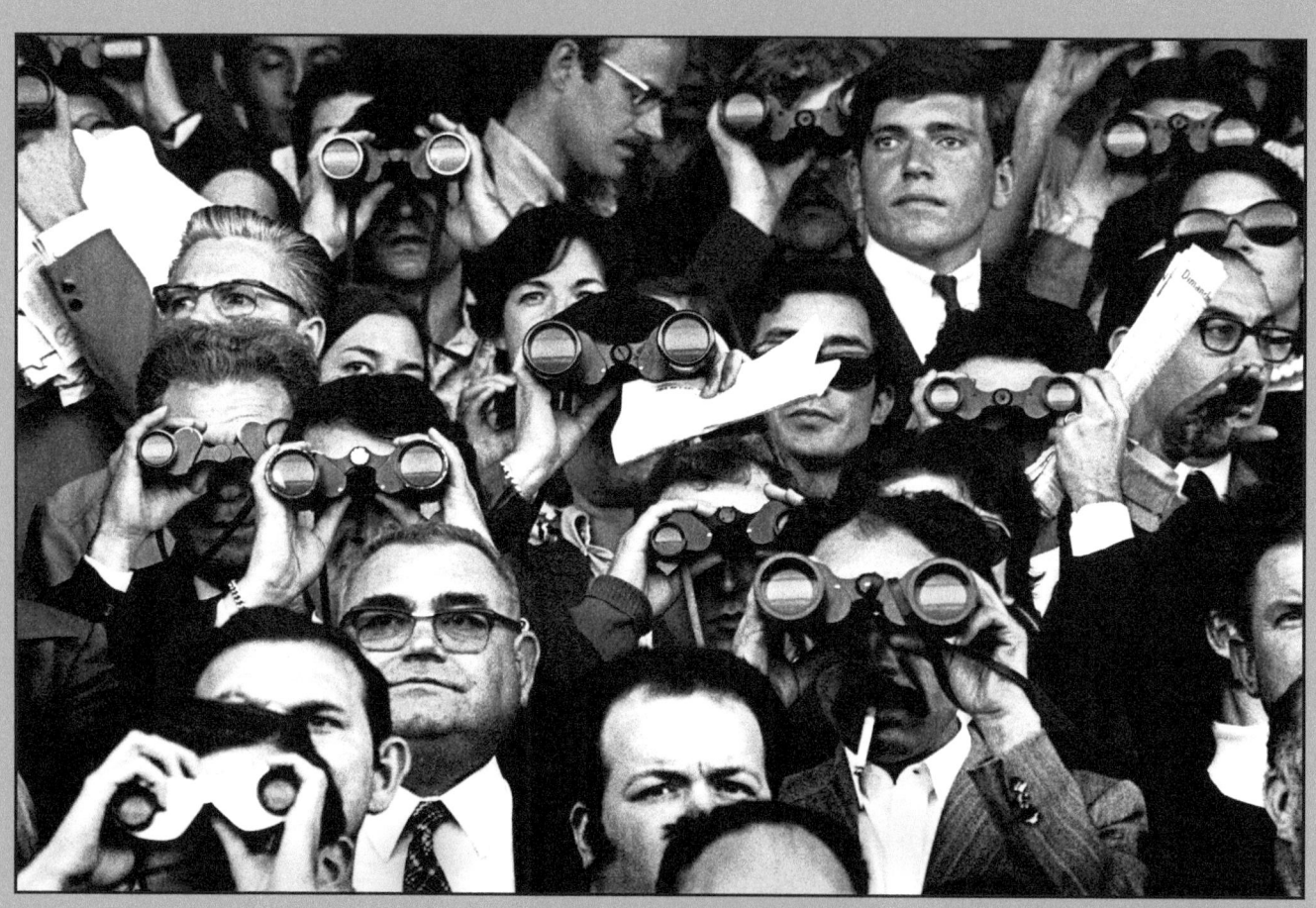

Paris, France - Longchamp Racecourse 1972

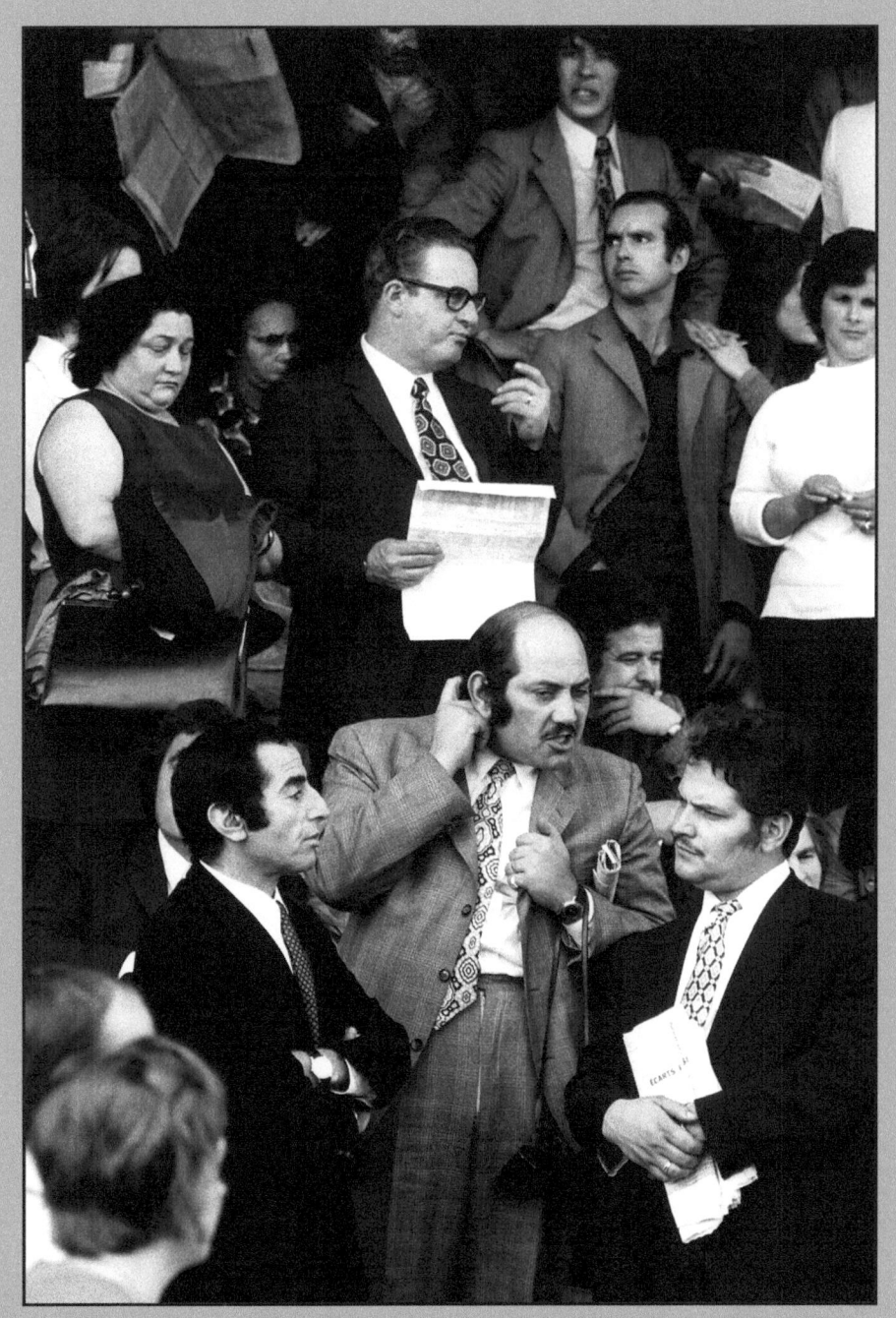

Paris, France - Longchamp Racecourse 1972

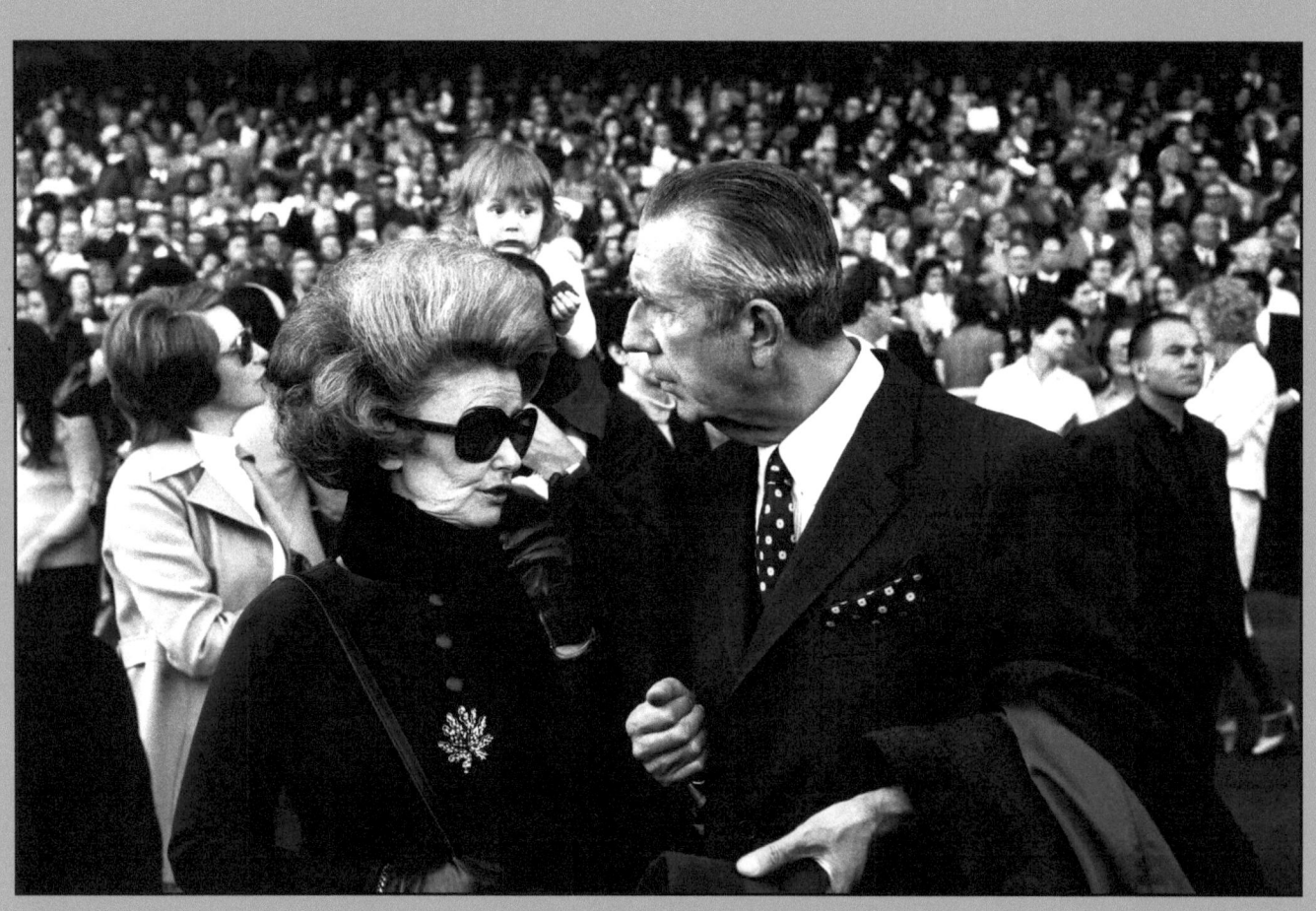

Paris, France - Longchamp Racecourse 1972

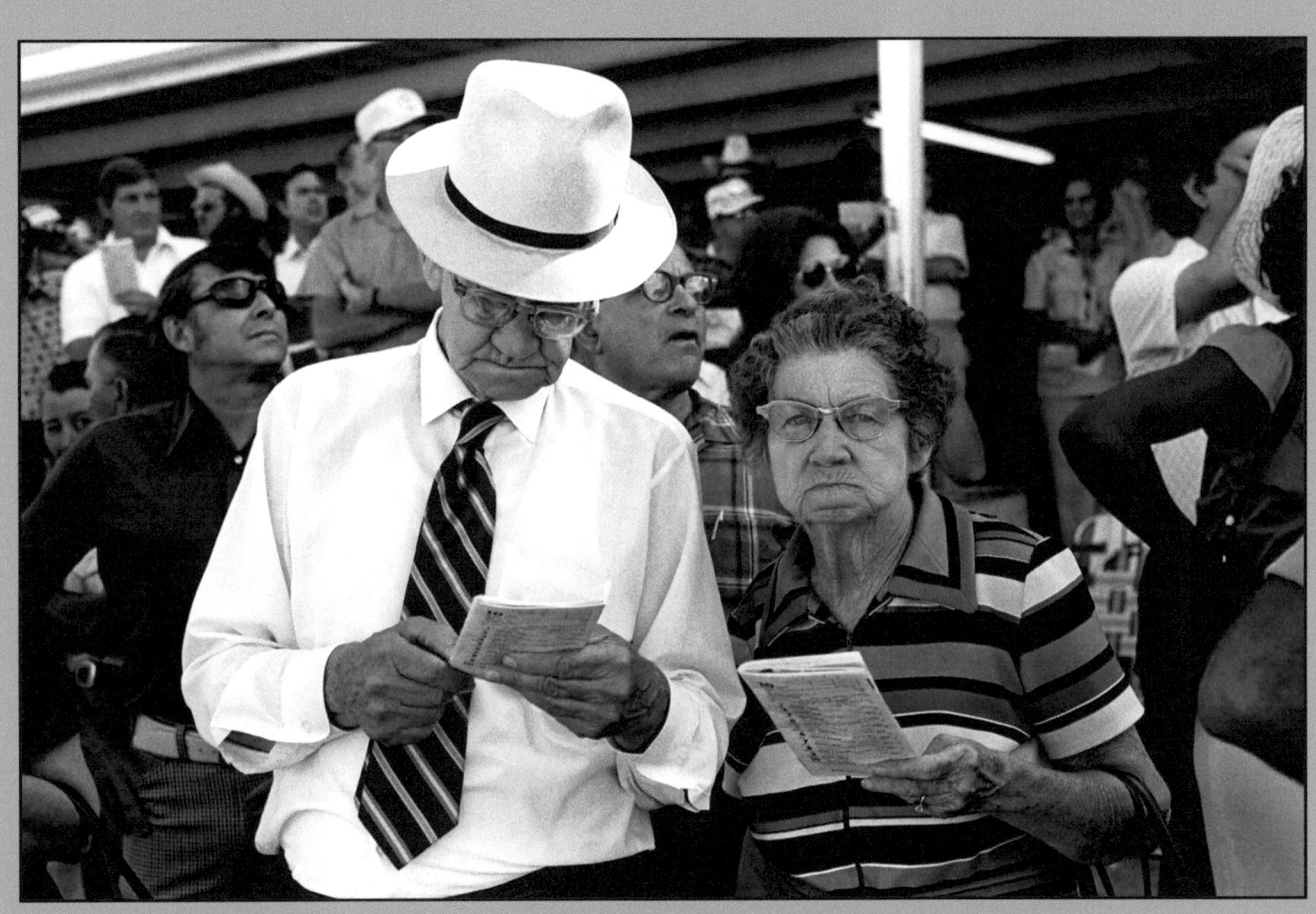
Lafayette, Louisiana - Evangeline Downs Race Track 1973

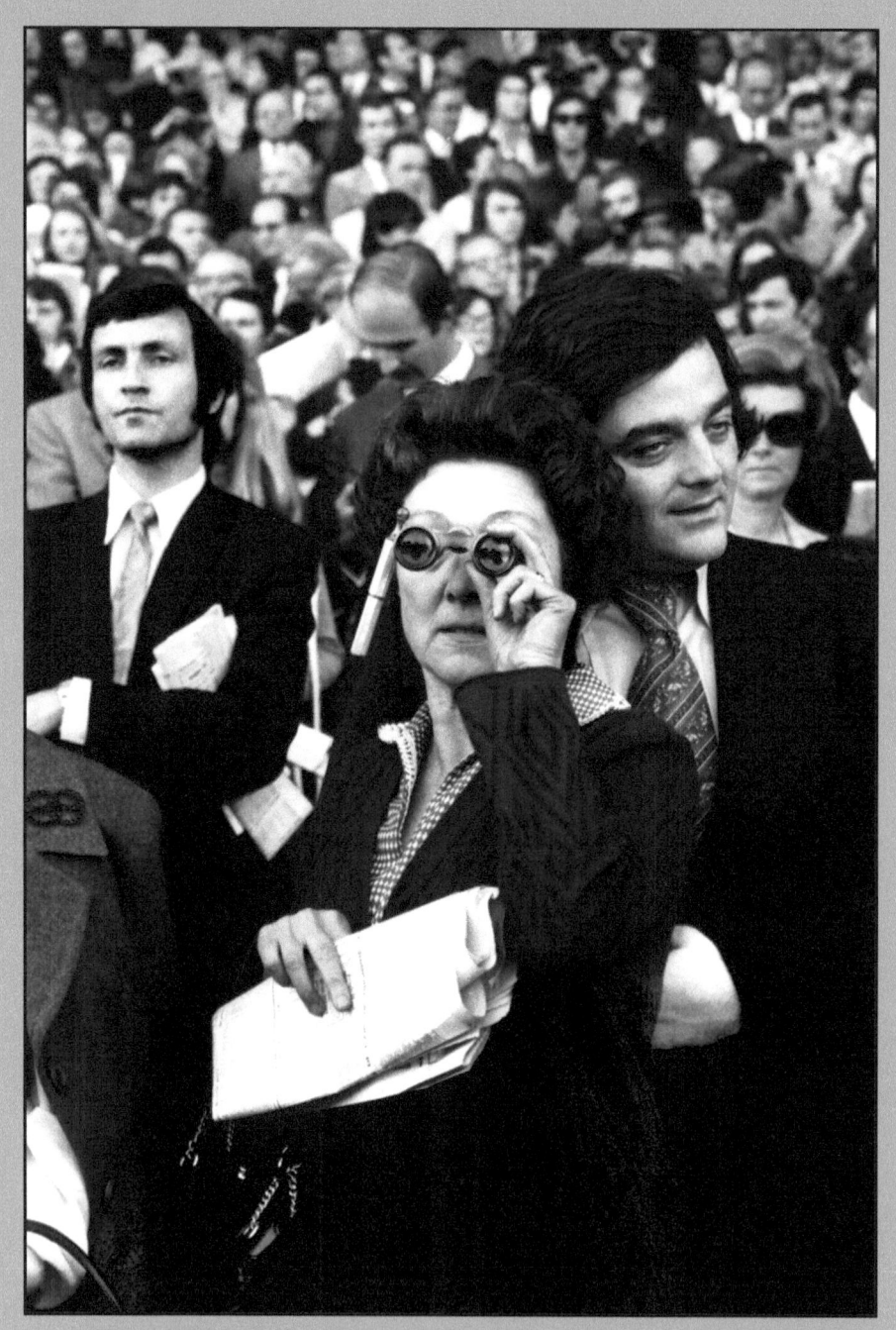
Paris, France - Longchamp Racecourse 1972

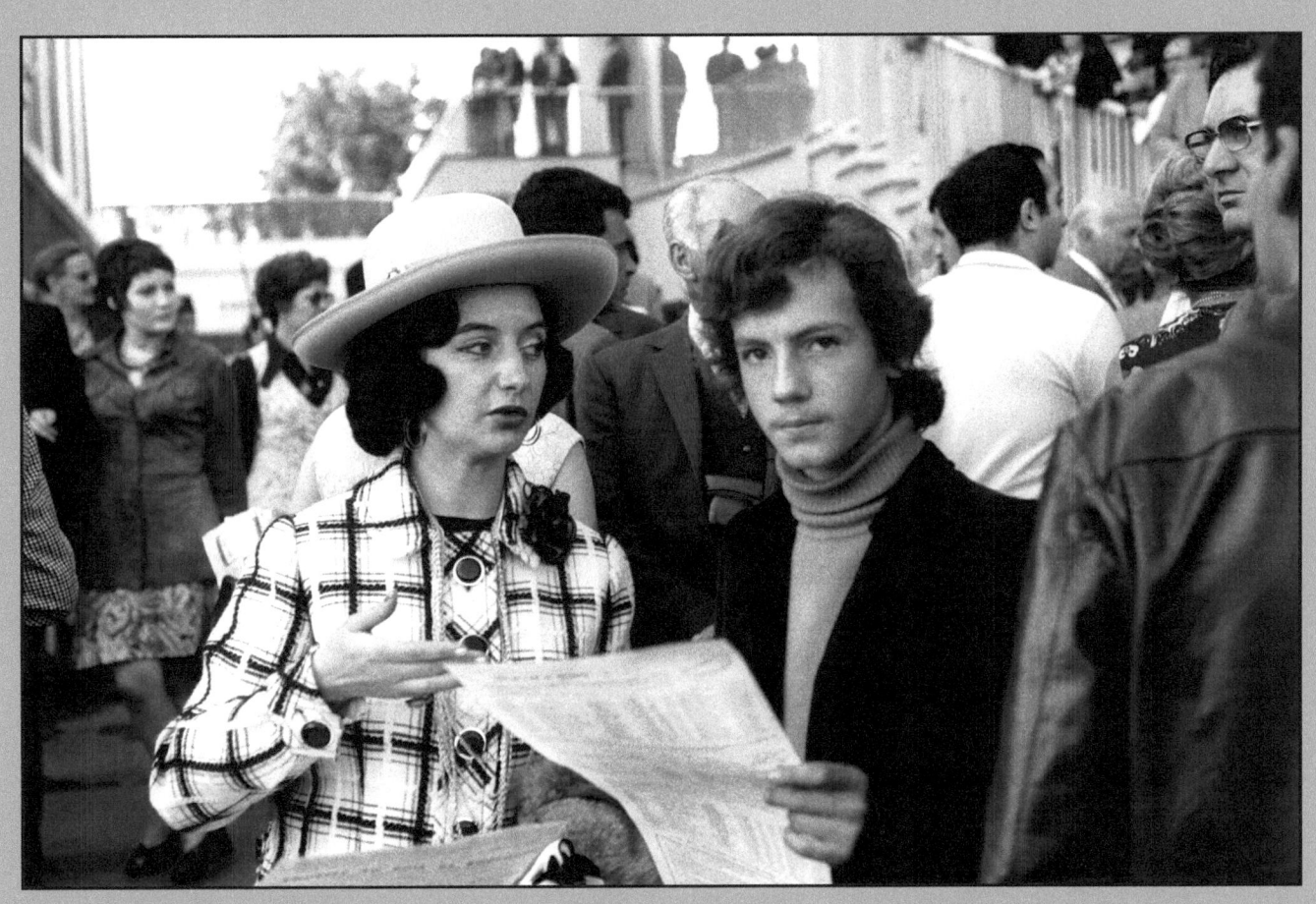

Paris, France - Longchamp Racecourse 1972

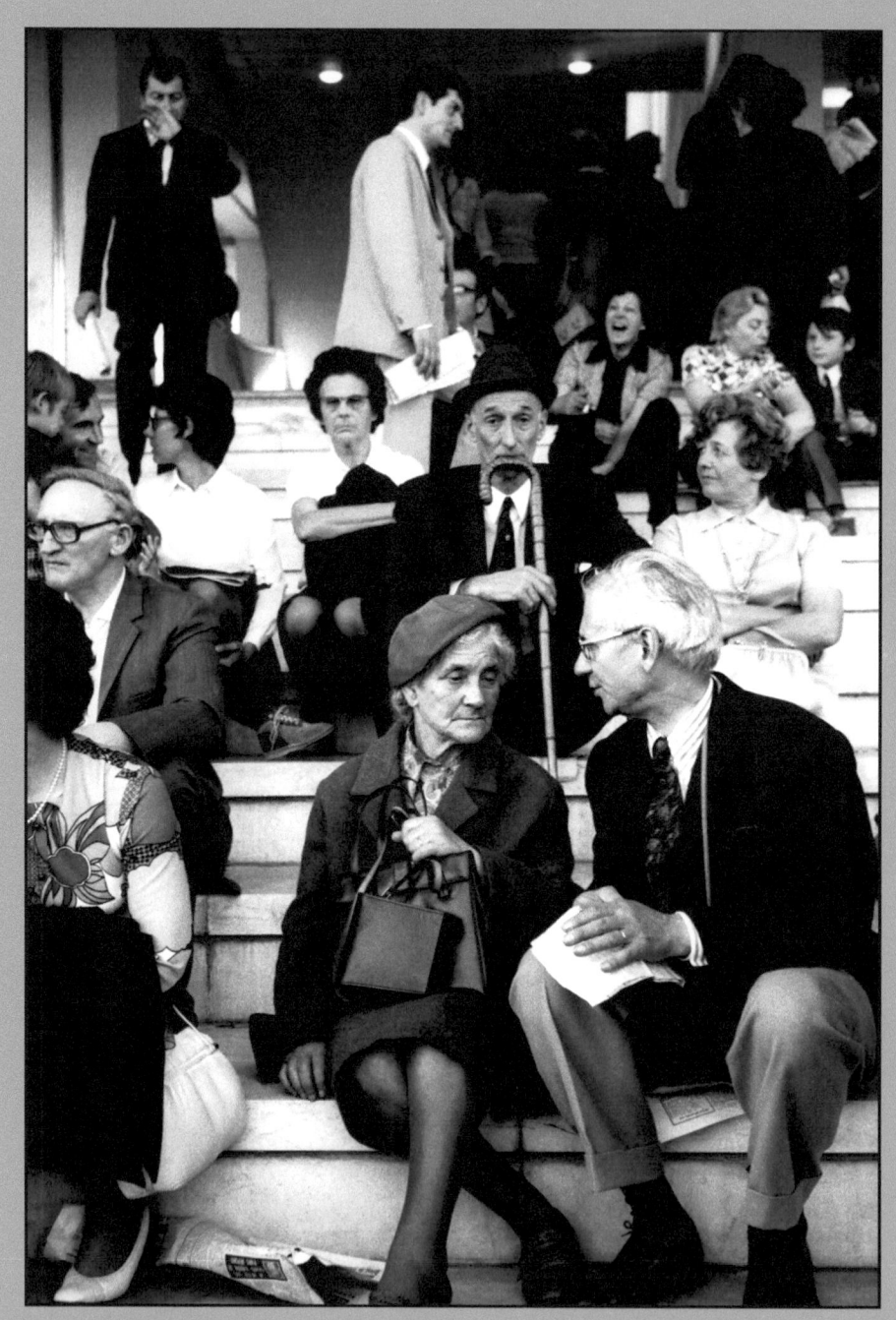

Paris, France - Longchamp Racecourse 1972

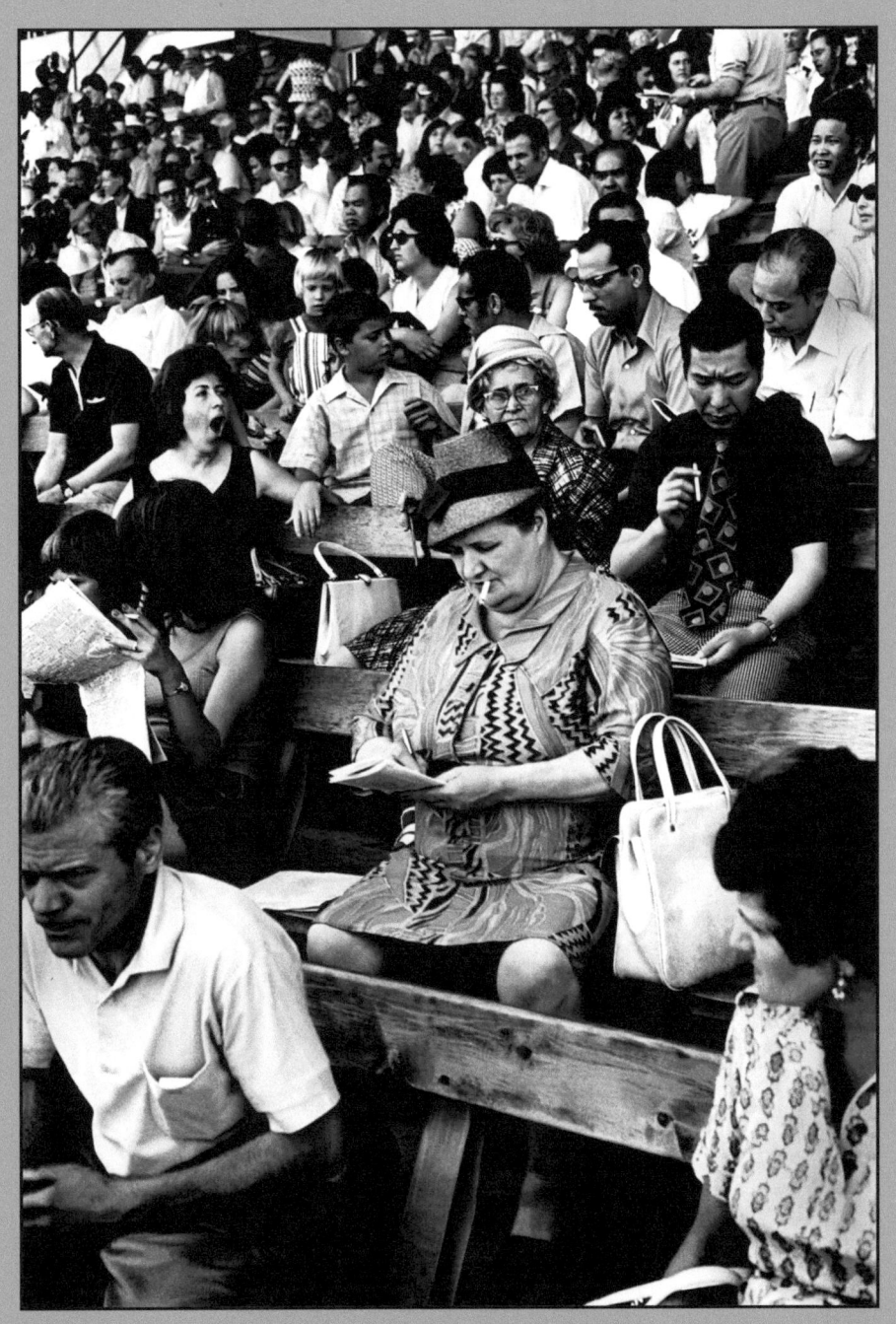

Vancouver, B.C., Canada - Exhibition Park/Hastings Racecourse 1973

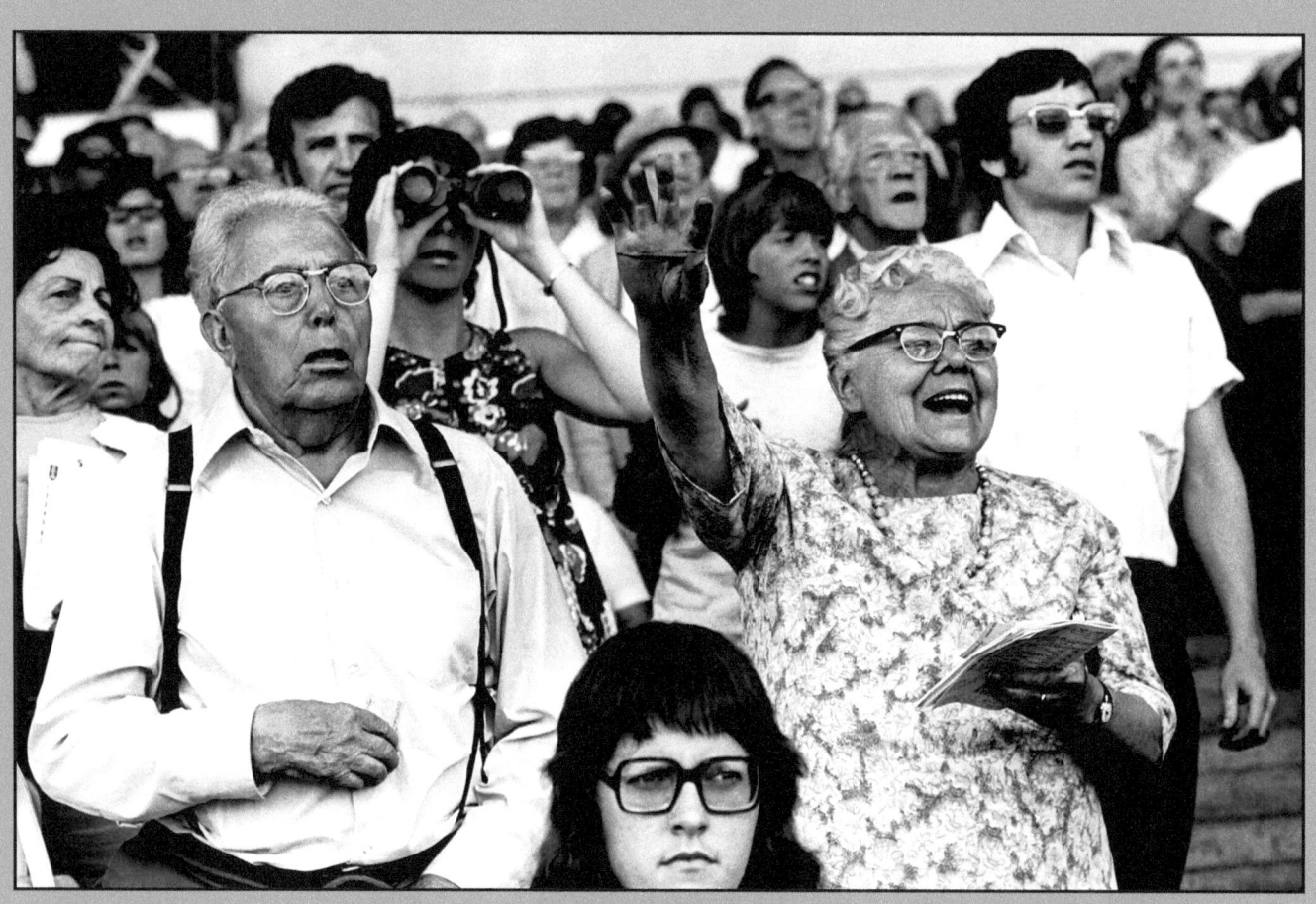

Vancouver, B.C., Canada - Exhibition Park/Hastings Racecourse 1973

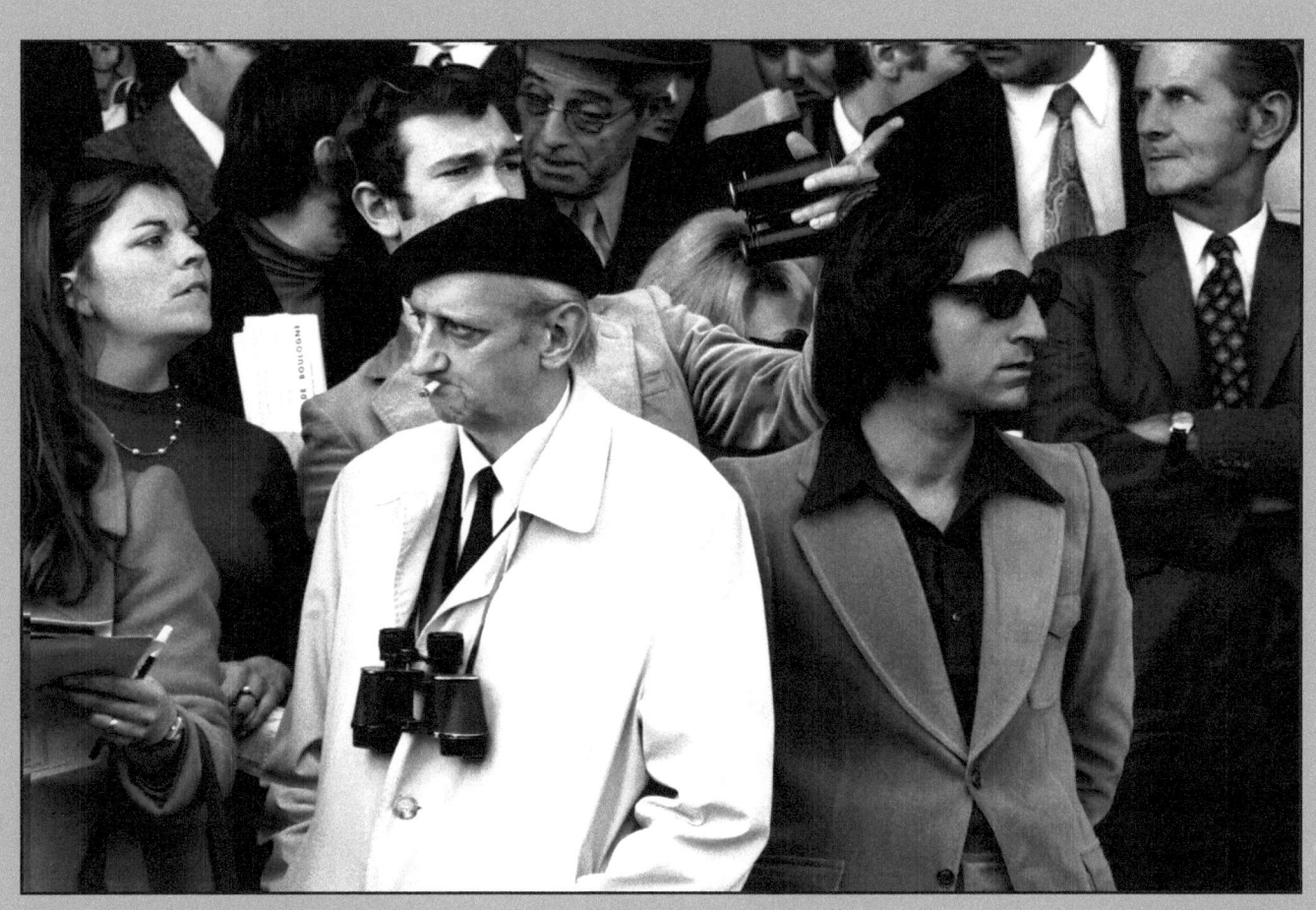

Paris, France - Longchamp Racecourse 1972

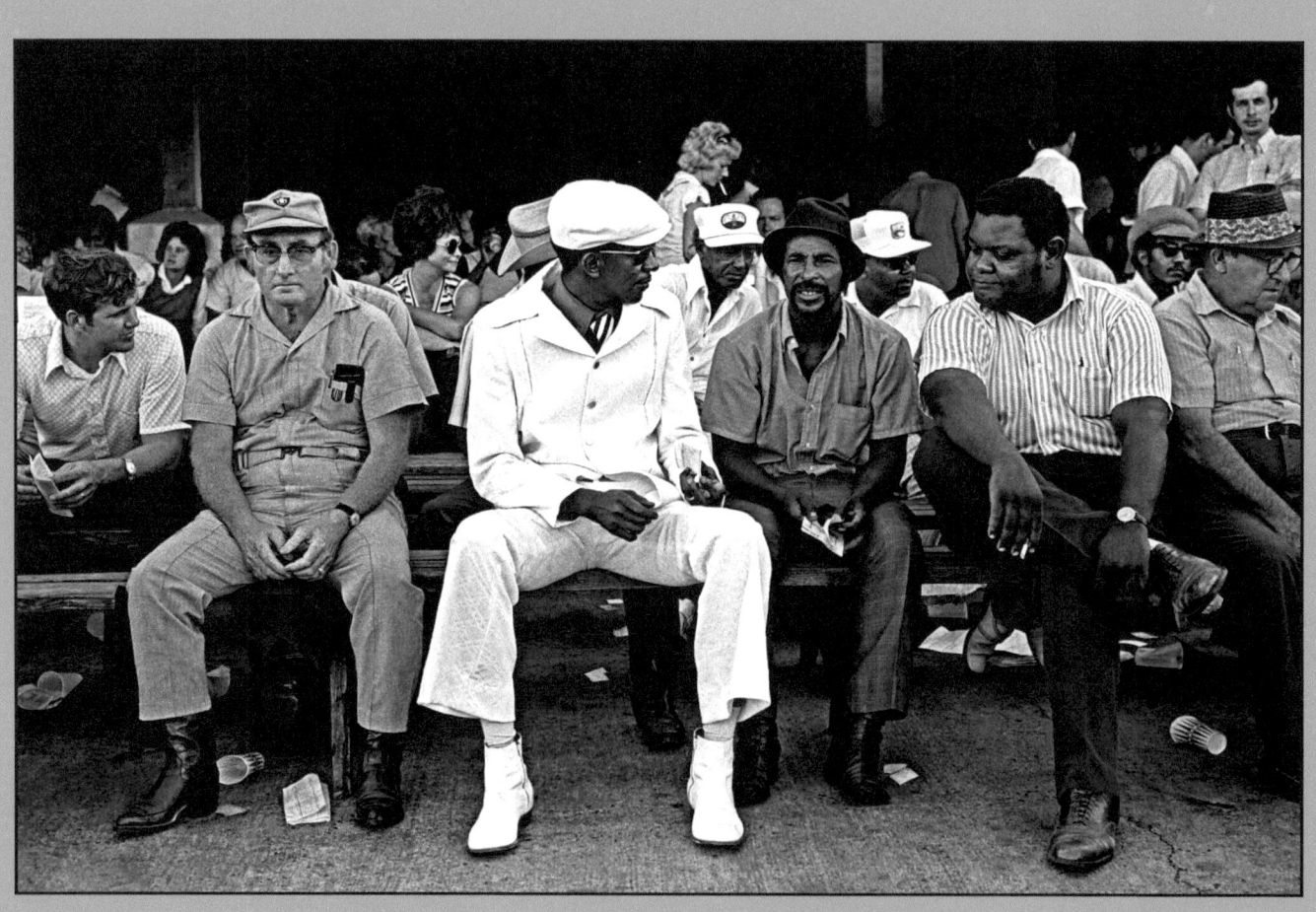

Lafayette, Louisiana - Evangeline Downs Race Track 1973

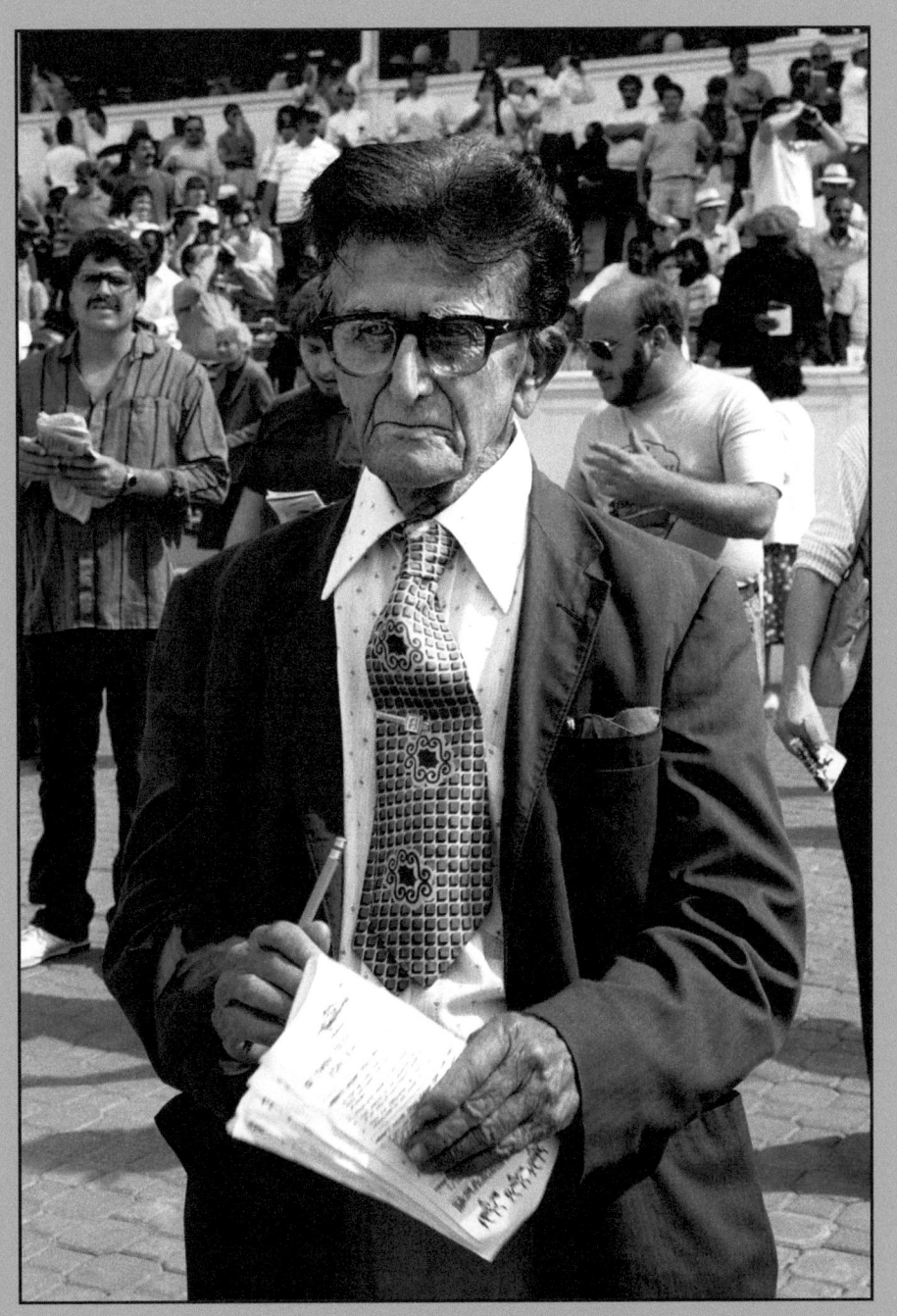

New Orleans, Louisiana - Fairground Race Track 1989

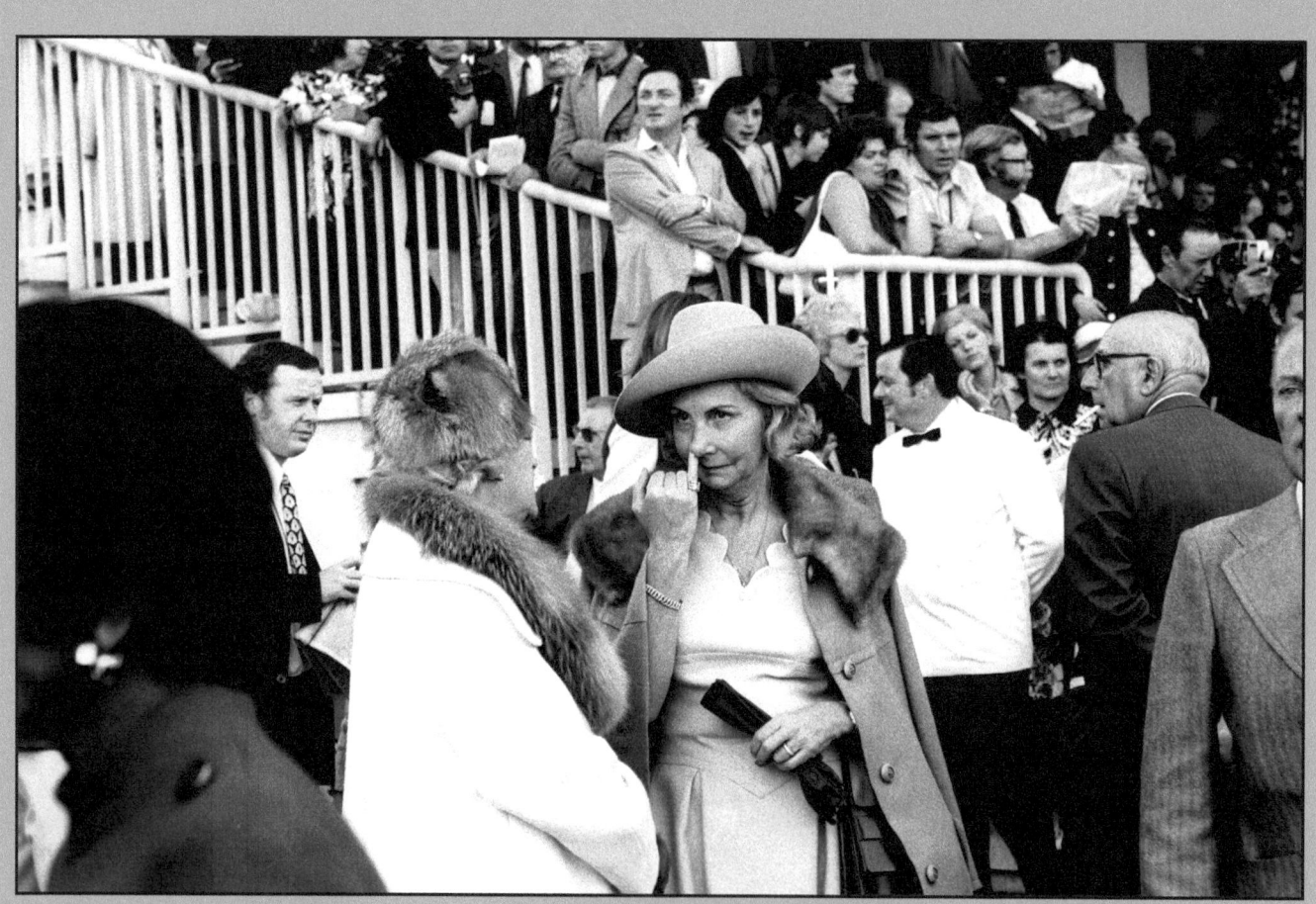

Paris, France - Longchamp Racecourse 1972

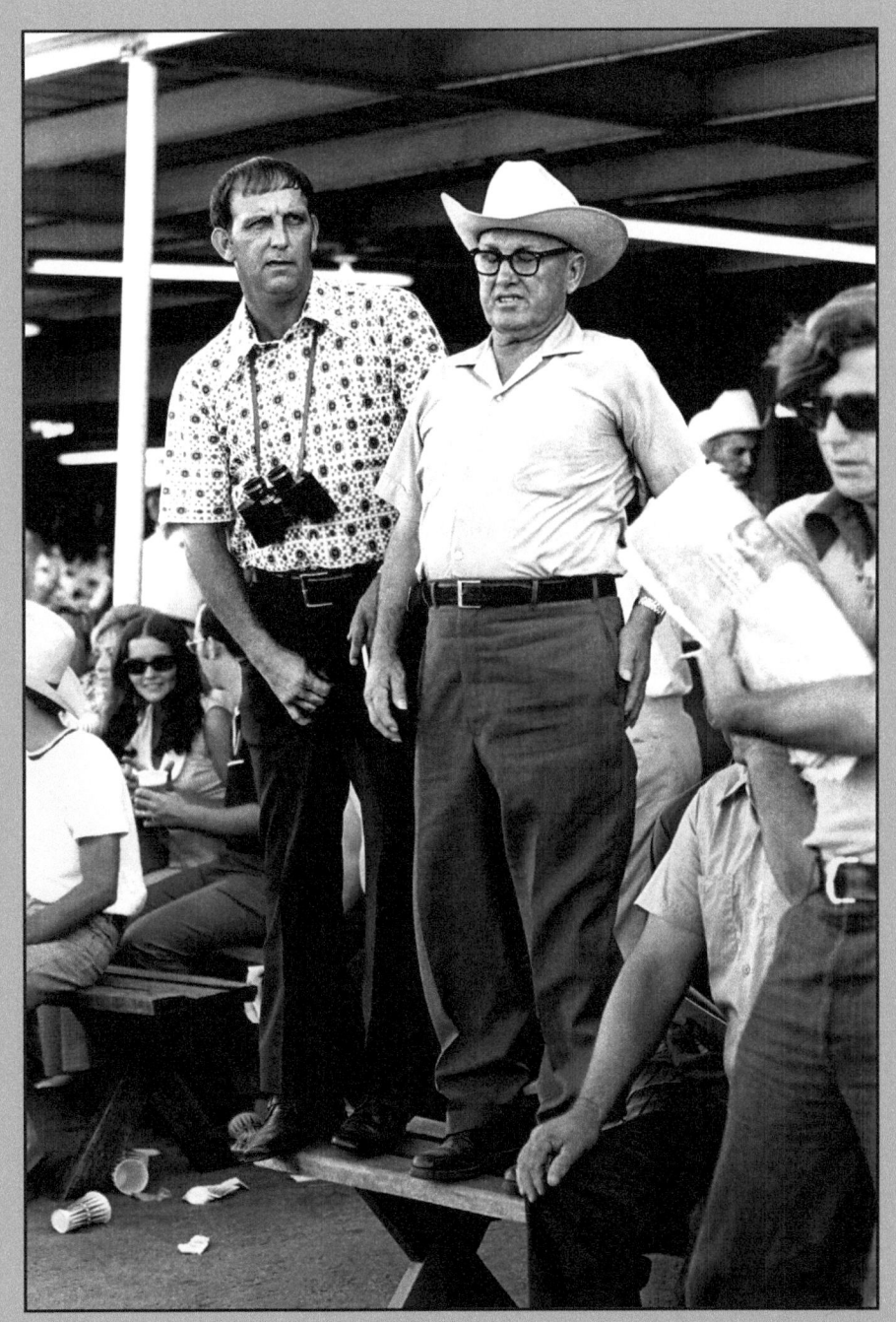

Lafayette, Louisiana - Evangeline Downs Race Track 1973

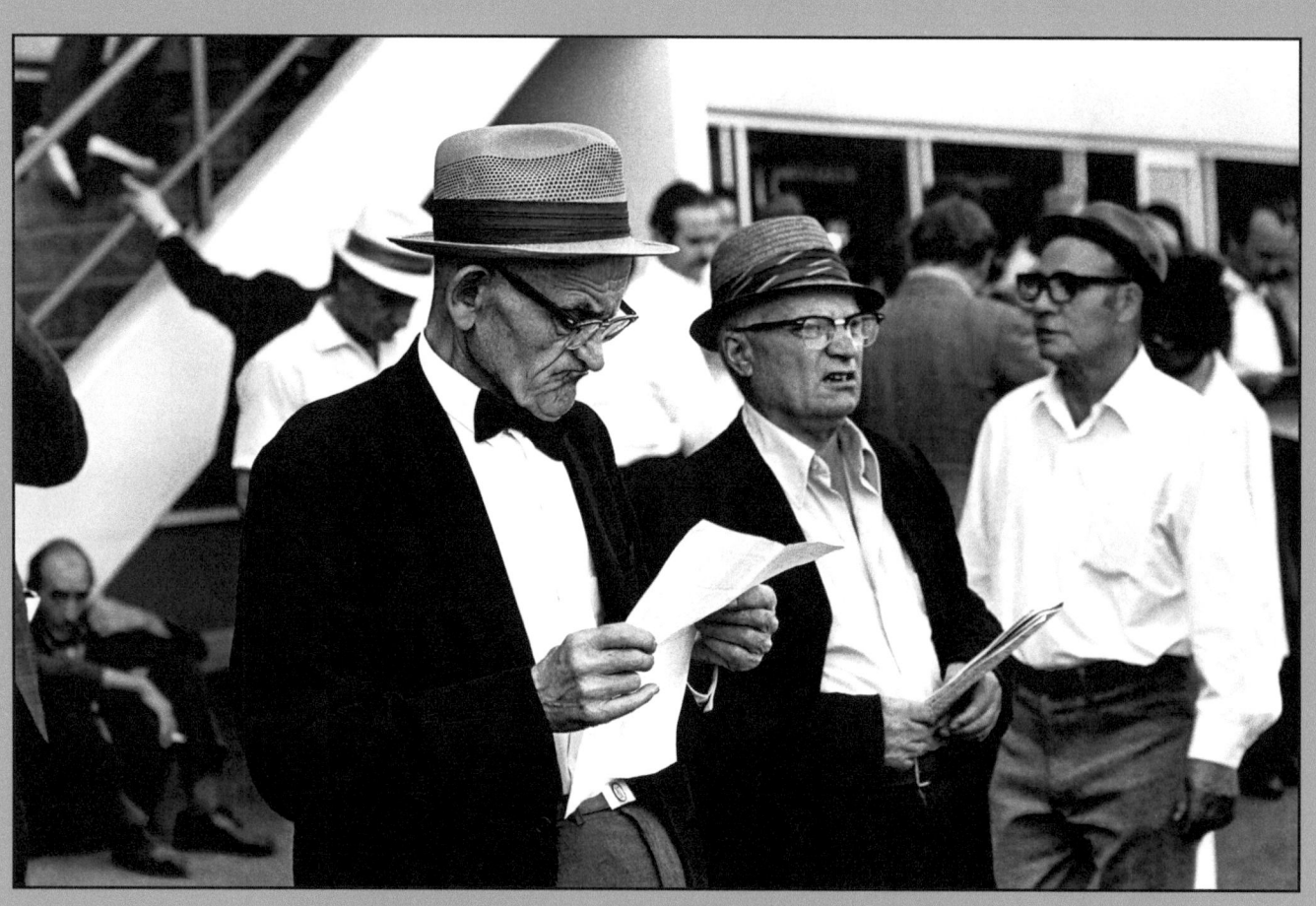

Vancouver, B.C., Canada - Exhibition Park/Hastings Racecourse 1973

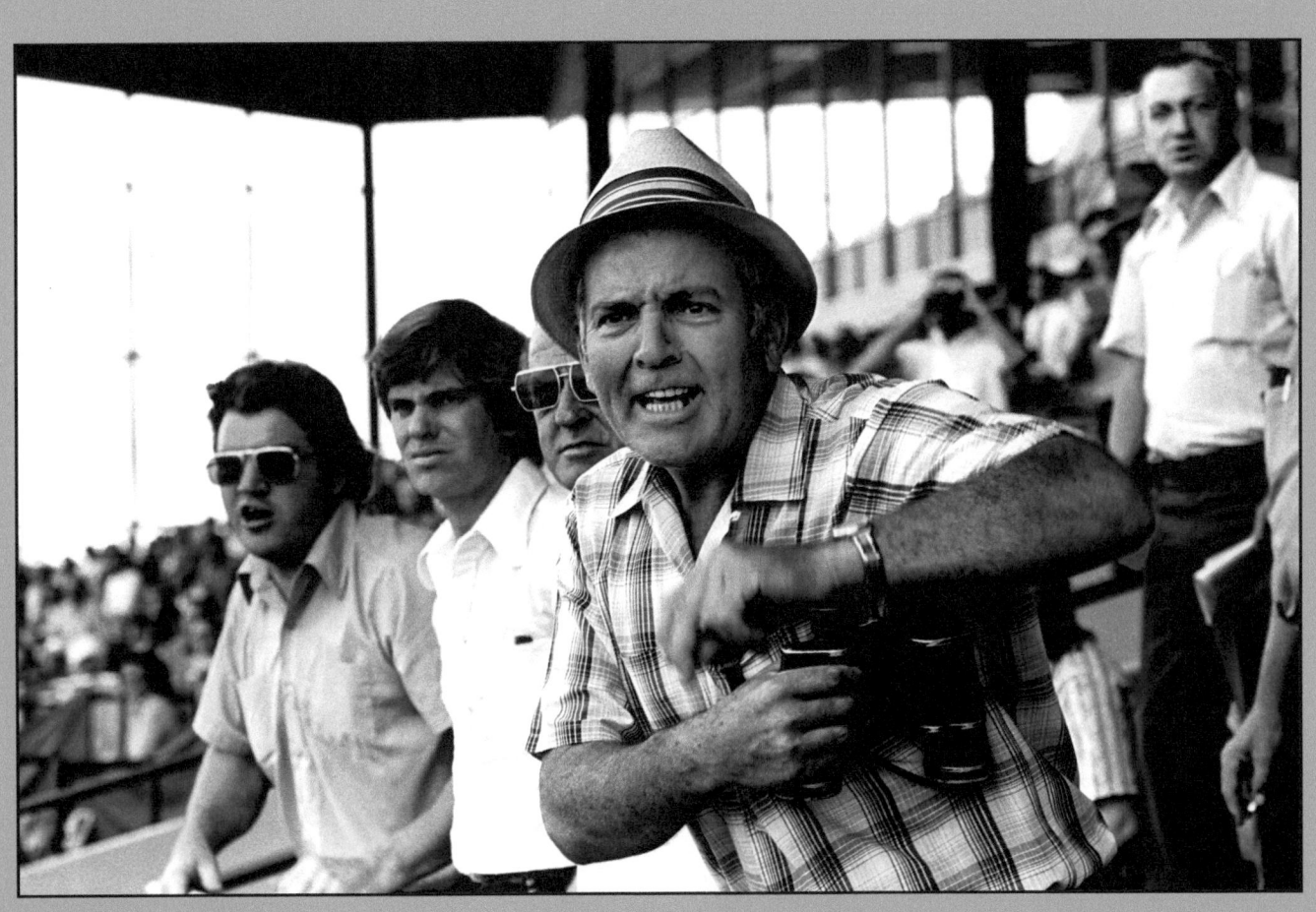
Vancouver, B.C., Canada - Exhibition Park/Hastings Racecourse 1973

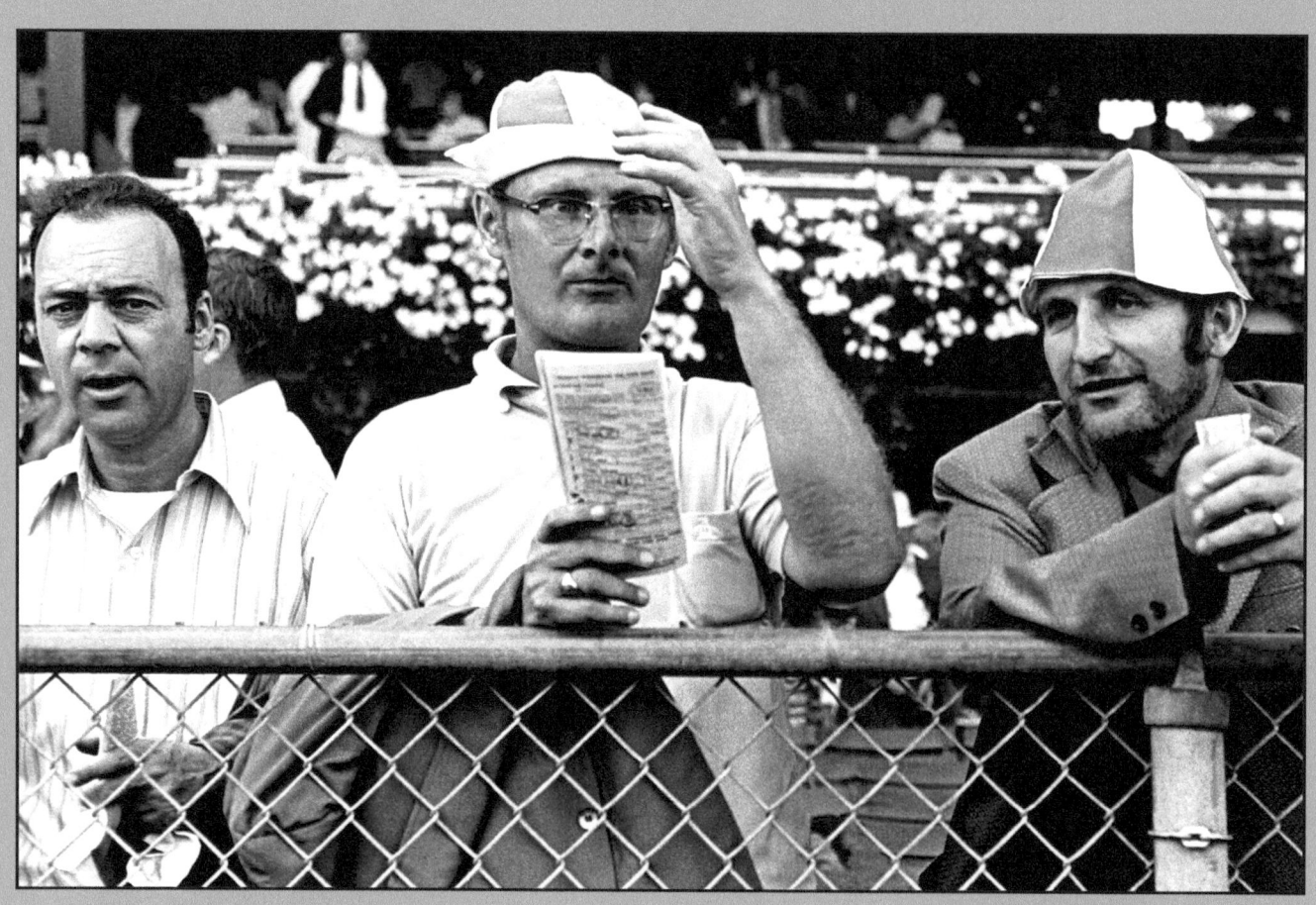

Saratoga Springs, New York - Saratoga Race Course 1973

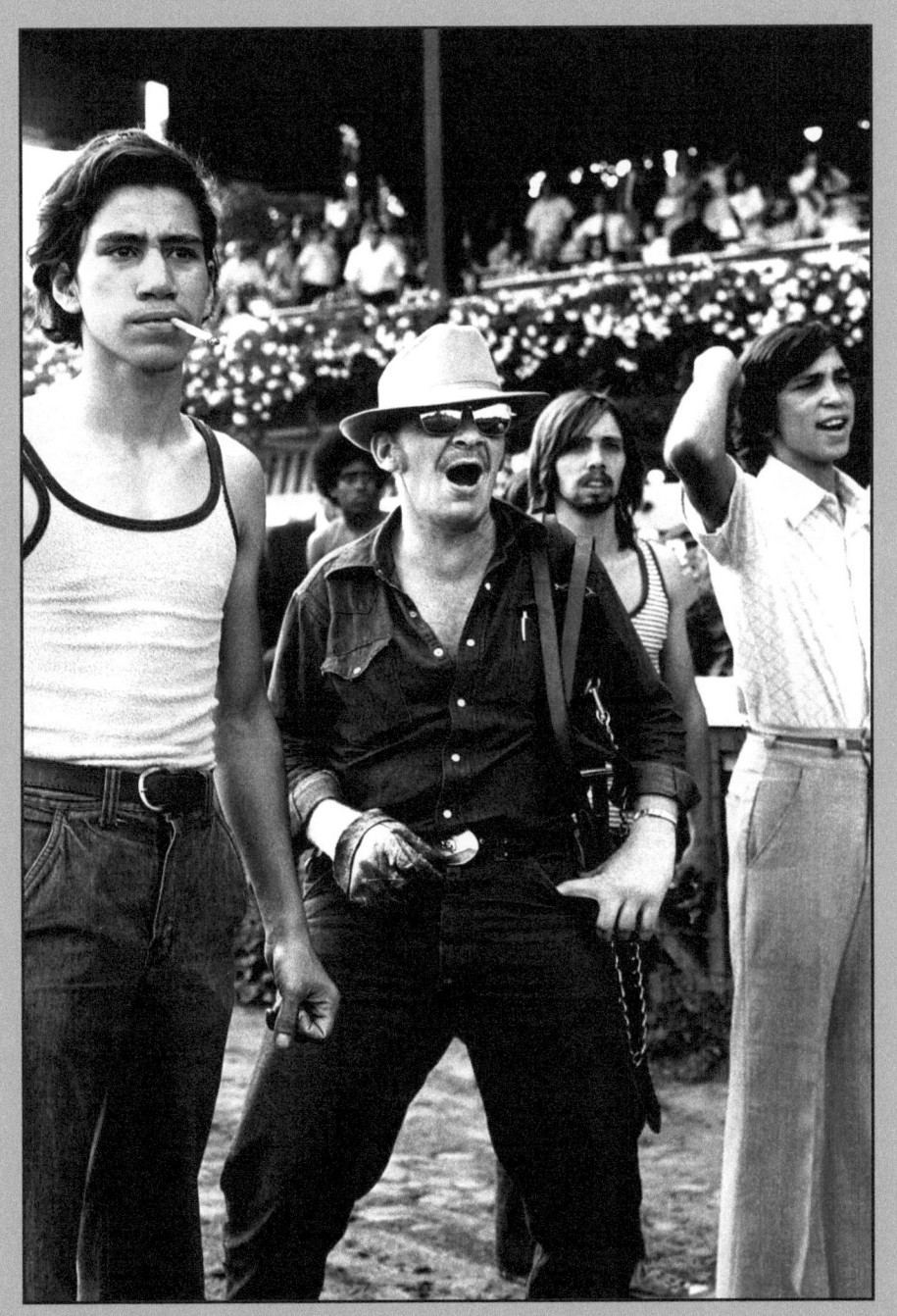
Saratoga Springs, New York - Saratoga Race Course 1973

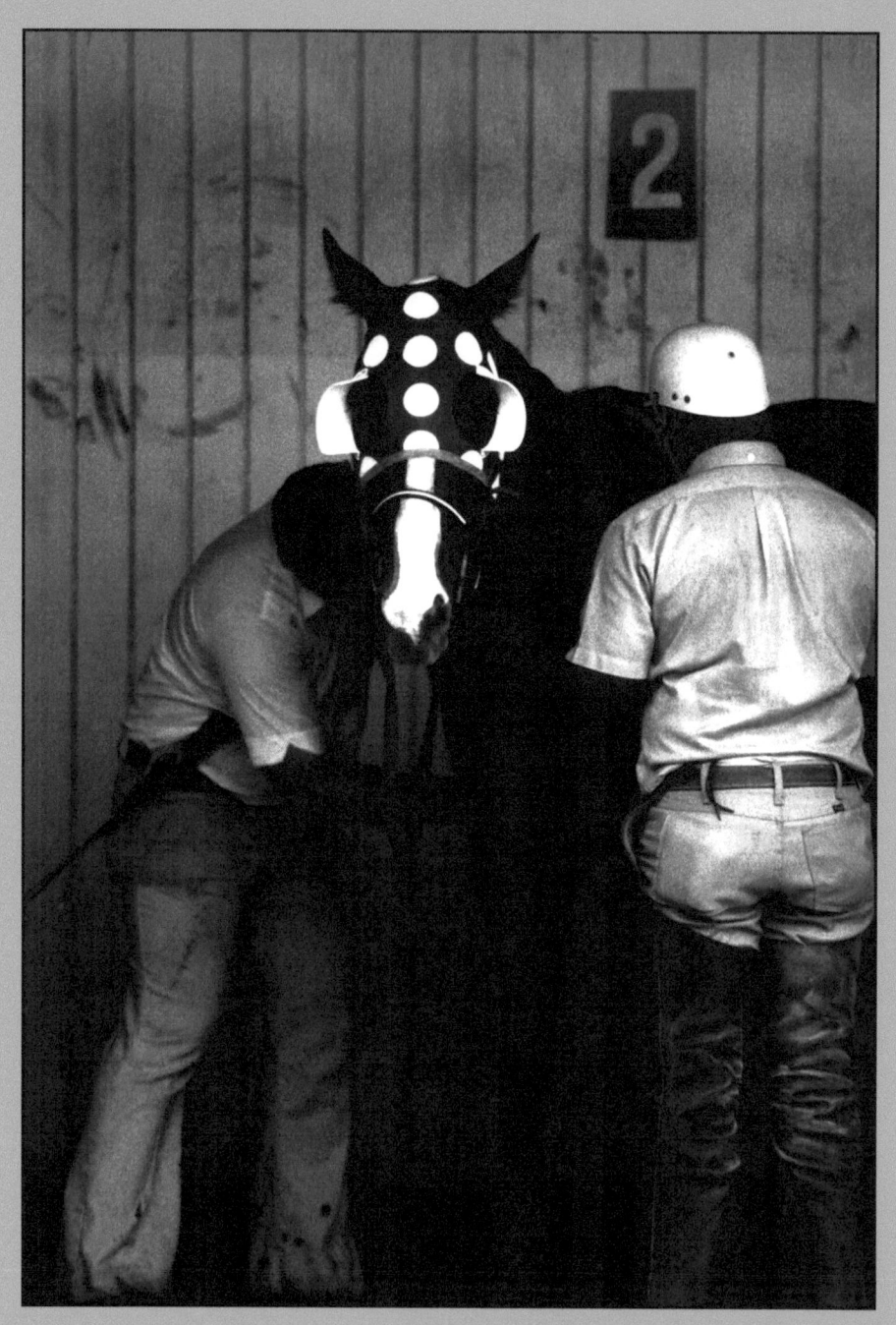
Lafayette, Louisiana - Evangeline Downs Race Track 1973

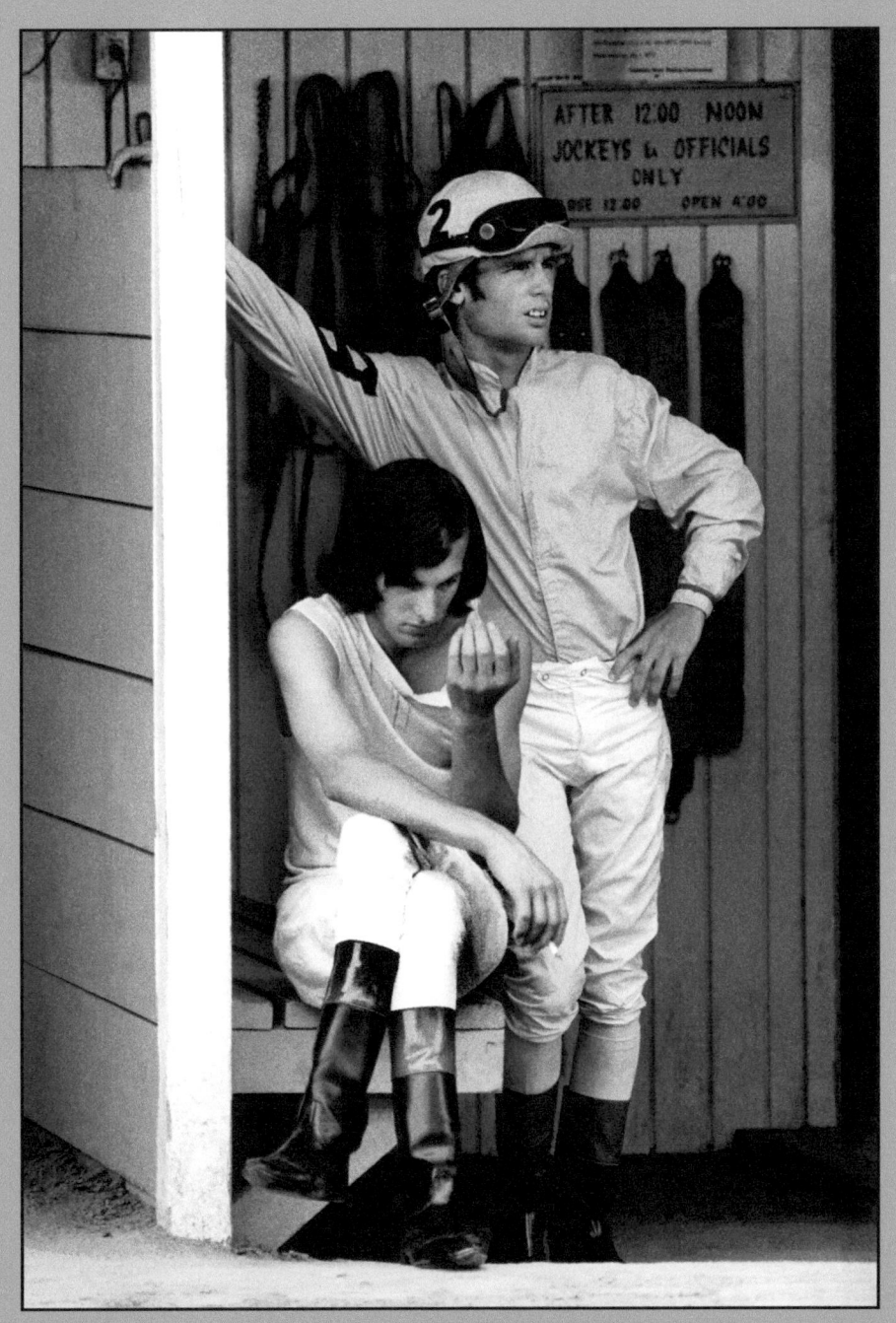

Lafayette, Louisiana - Evangeline Downs Race Track 1973

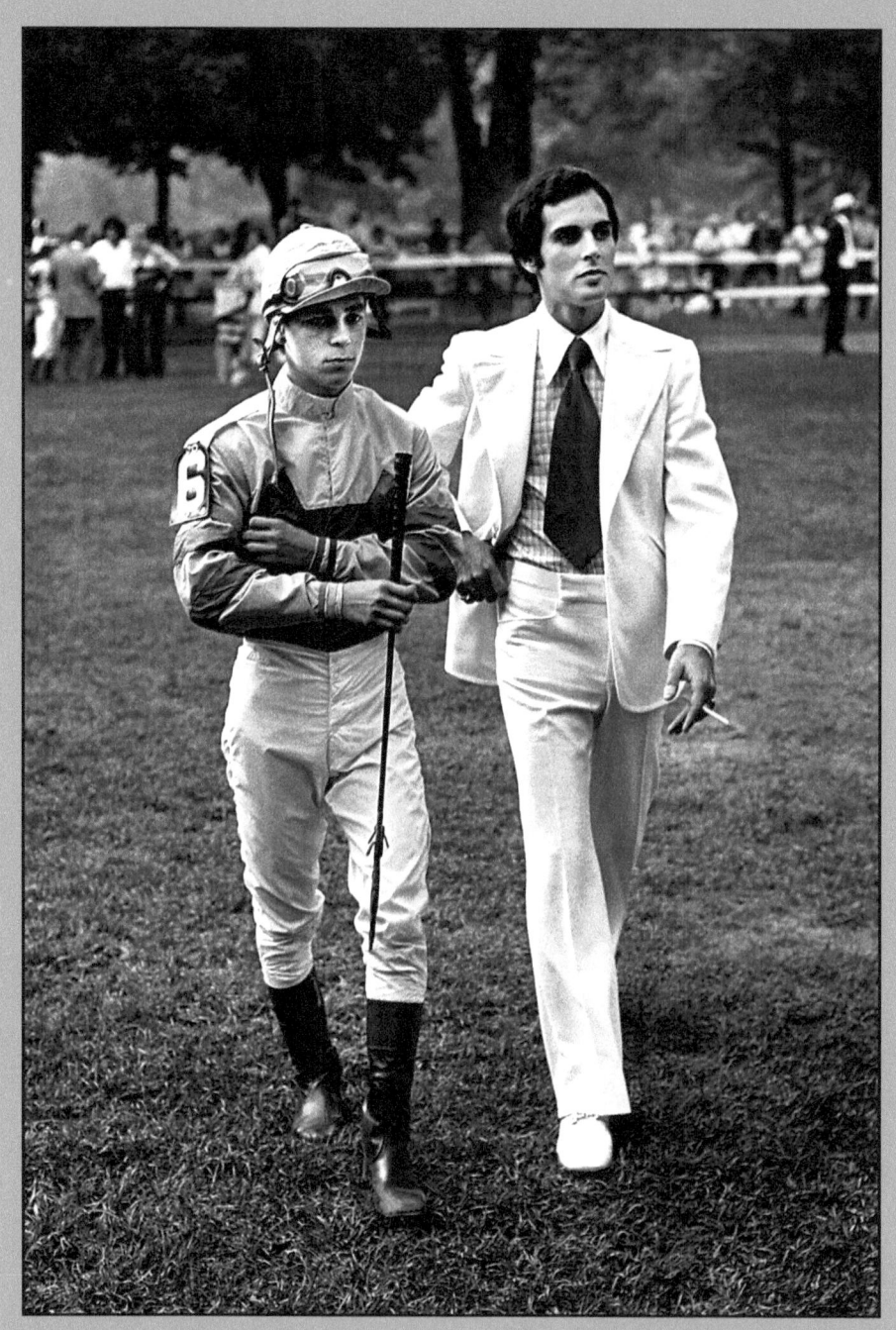

Saratoga Springs, New York - Saratoga Race Course 1973

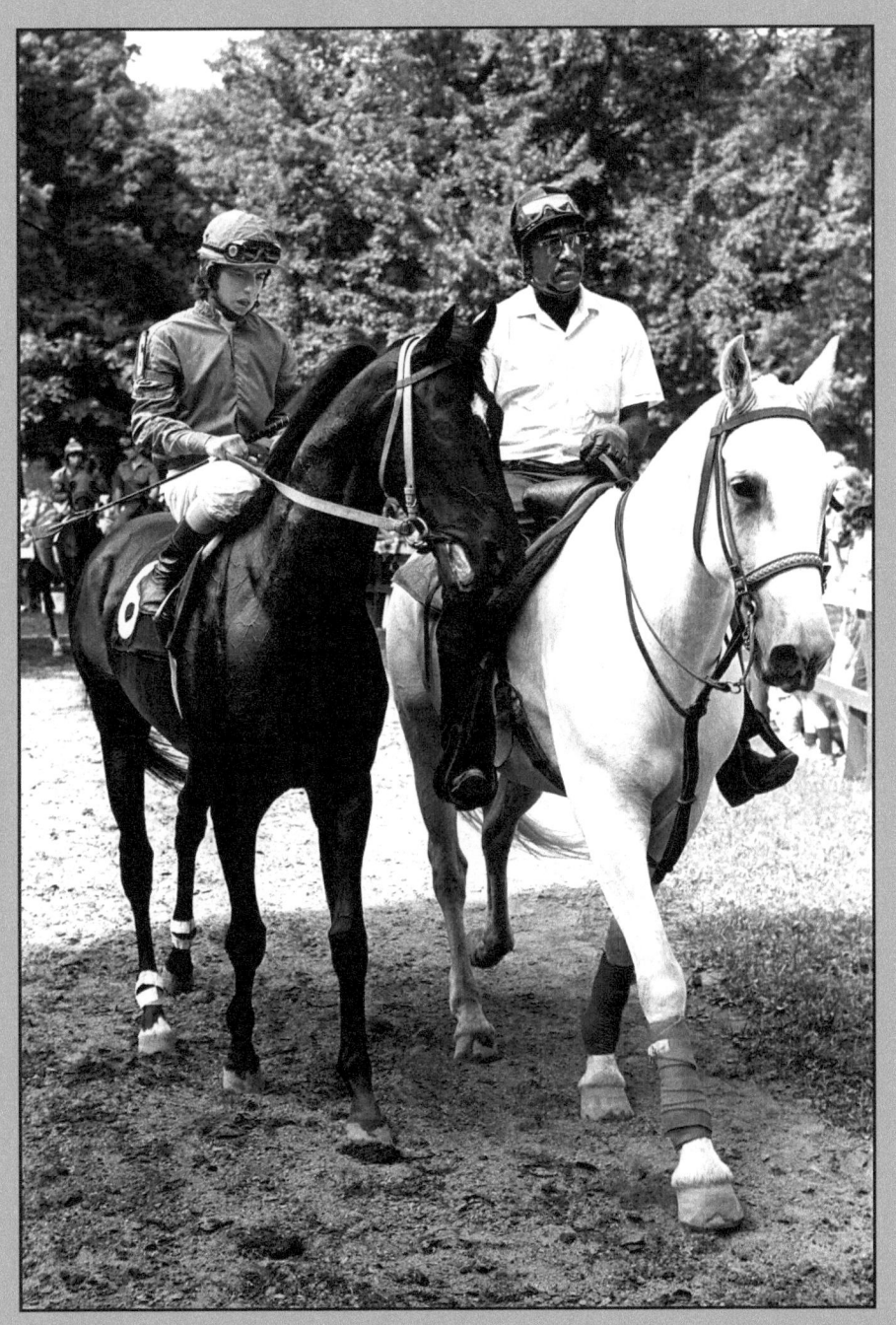

Saratoga Springs, New York - Saratoga Race Course 1973

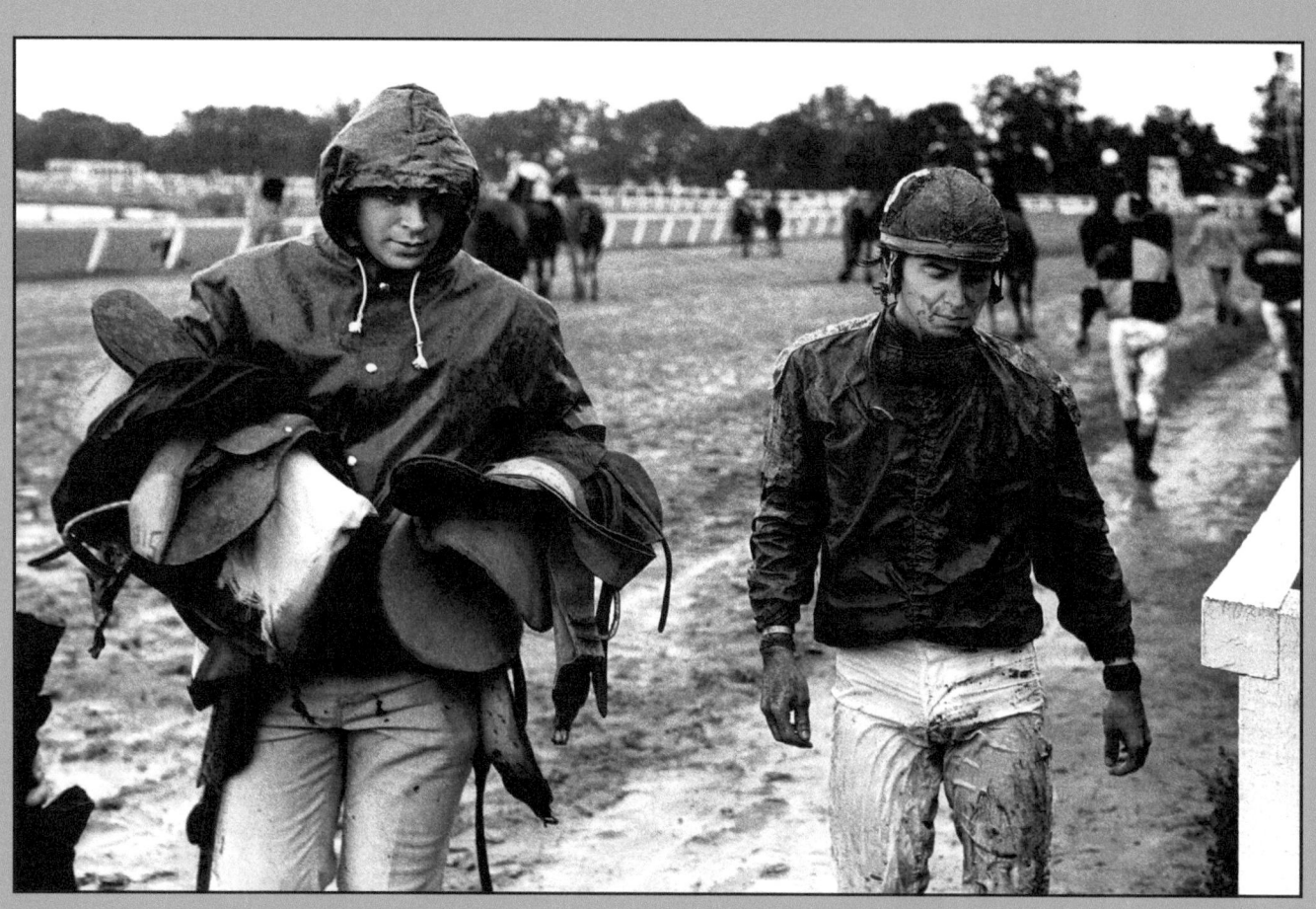

Lafayette, Louisiana - Evangeline Downs Race Track 1973

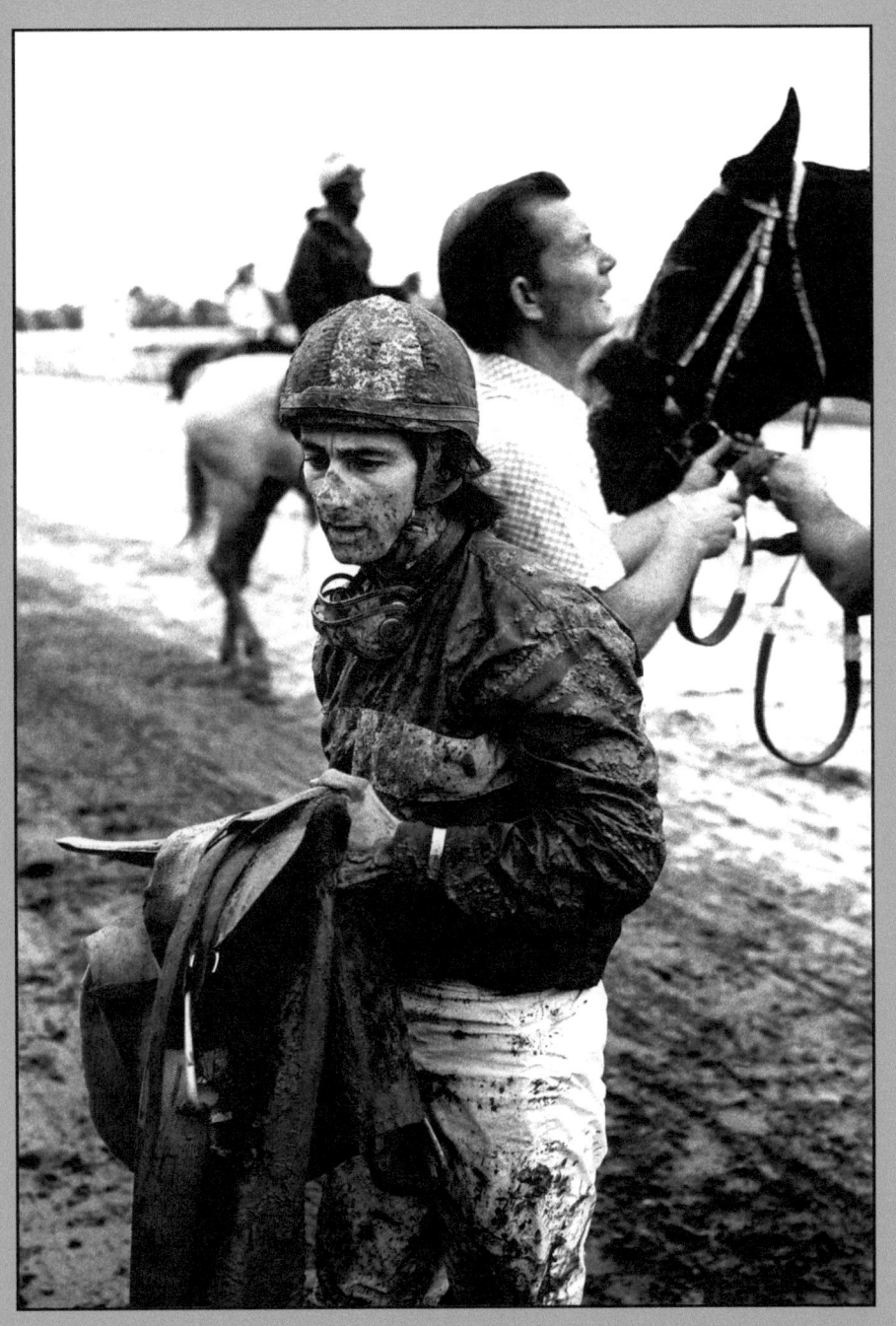

Lafayette, Louisiana - Evangeline Downs Race Track 1973

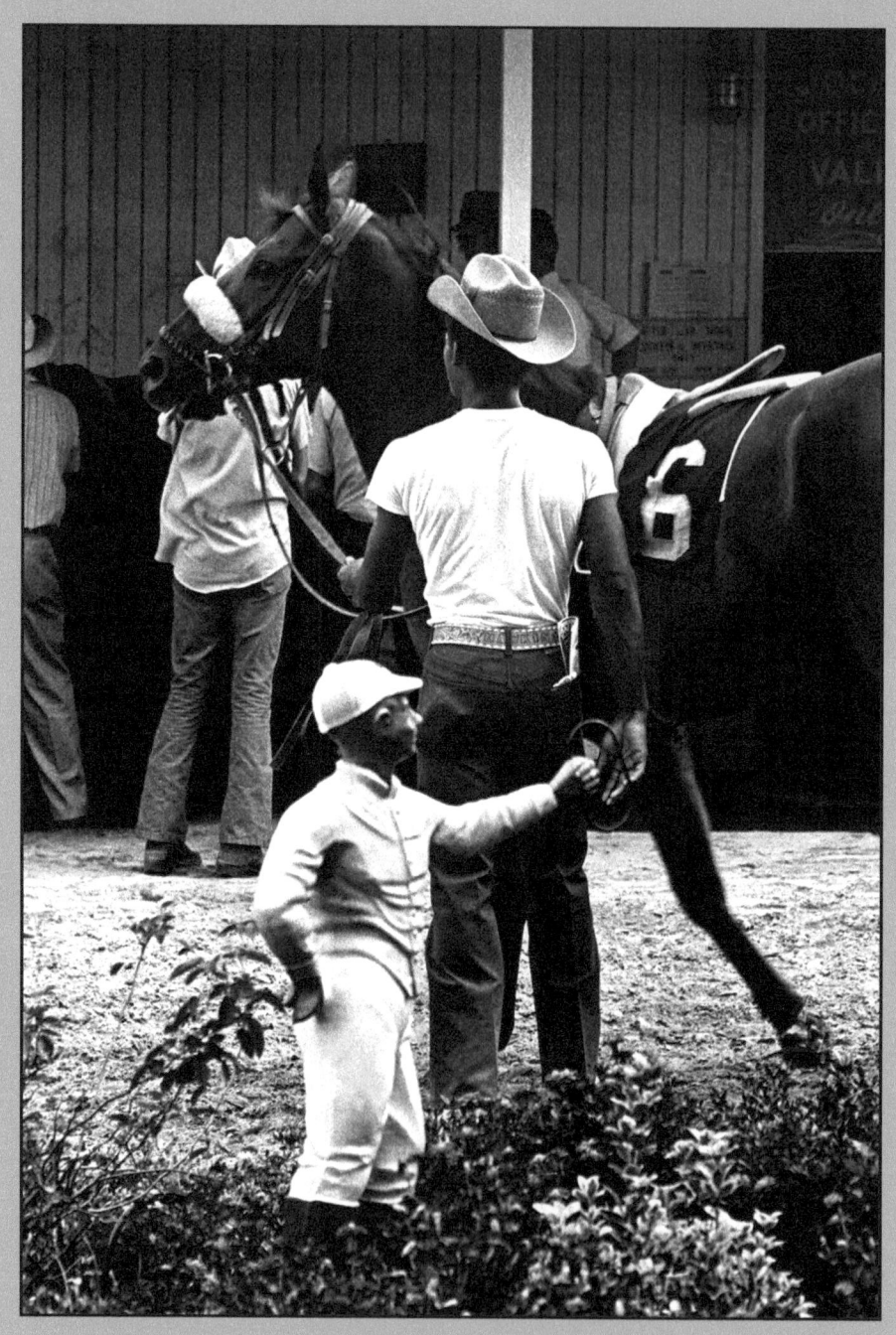

Lafayette, Louisiana - Evangeline Downs Race Track 1973

Thanks for coming to the races
I hope you left winning

Photographer Bio

BOOKS: *REJOICE WHEN YOU DIE - The New Orleans Jazz Funerals (LSU Press 1998).*
DUET - Poet & Photographer - Elizabeth Burk & Leo Touchet (Yellow Flag Press 2018)
PEOPLE AMONG US - Photography by Leo Touchet
CHASING SHADOWS - Desert Sand Dunes
FLOWERS - In Black & White

COLLECTIONS: Sir Elton John Photography Collection, New Orelans Museum of Art, Houston Museum of Fine Arts, Bibliotheque National (France), Everson Museum of Art, Schomburg Center (New York Public Library), Chase Manhattan Collection, U.S. National Park Service.

PUBLICATIONS: Life Magazine, Time Magazine, Time Life Books, National Geographic Books, Newsweek Magazine, Fortune Magazine, Natural History Magazine, New York Times, Washington Post, Boston Globe, Oxford American Magazine, Southern Quarterly, Southern Living Magazine, America Illustrated (USIA), Der Stern (Germany), Panorama (Italy), Popular Photography.

EXHIBITIONS: Acadiana Center for the Arts, Arizona State University, Arkansas Art Center, Brooks Memorial (Memphis), Columbus Musuem (Georgia), Everson Museum (Syracuse), Fotofest '92 (Houston), Hofstra University (New York), Louisiana State University, Miami Art Center, Mint Museum (North Carolina), Mississippi Southern University, New Orleans Public Library, Oklahoma Art Center, Public Theater (New York City), Royal Ontario Museum (Toronto), University of Houston, University of Oklahoma, University of Texas.

GROUP EXHIBITIONS:
REGARDS et MEMOIRES - ARLES 2008 - 39th Annual Arles, France Photo Expo
   (Four Exhibitions including Public Street Banners on the rue de la Roquette)
PHOTOGRAPHY USA 1976, United States Bicentennial Exhibition
   (USIA exhibition circulated in the Soviet Union and East Europe).

Leo Touchet's Website: www.leotouchet.com
For print sales: Contact Coco Conroy
coco@jacksonfineart.com
Jackson Fine Art Gallery in Atlanta, Georgia

Other Photo Books by
LEO TOUCHET

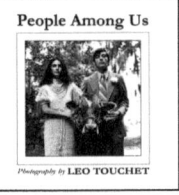

People Among Us - *Photography by Leo Touchet*

ISBN: 9781732443303 - 8.5 x 8.5 inches - 46 Pages - Paperback
Black & white photographs of people around the world.

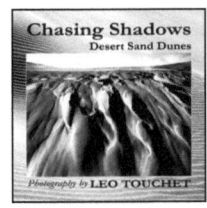

Chasing Shadows - *Desert Sand Dunes*

ISBN: 9781732443303 - 8.5 x 8.5 inches - 36 Pages - Paperback
Black & white photographs of desert sand dunes.

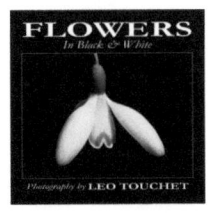

Flowers - *In Black & White*

ISBN: 9781732443334 - 8.5 x 8.5 inches - 36 Pages - Paperback
Black & white photographs of flowers.

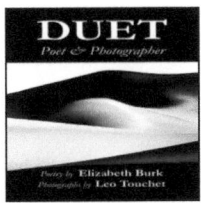

DUET - Poet & Photographer

Poet - **Elizabeth Burk**   *Photographer* - **Leo Touchet**
ISBN: 9781732443303 - 8.5 x 8.5 inches - 60 Pages - Paperback
Black & white photographs of desert sand dunes.

These books are available from:
www.photocirclepress.com

www.ingramcontent.com/pod-product-compliance
Lightning Source LLC
Chambersburg PA
CBHW040416220526
45473CB00004B/1265